Career Launcher

Computers and Programming

Career Launcher series

Advertising and Public Relations
Computers and Programming
Education
Energy
Fashion
Film
Finance
Food Services
Hospitality
Internet
Health Care Management
Health Care Providers
Law
Law Enforcement and Public Safety
Manufacturing
Nonprofit Organizations
Performing Arts
Professional Sports Organizations
Real Estate
Recording Industry
Television
Video Games

Career Launcher

Computers and Programming

Lisa McCoy

Ferguson Publishing
An imprint of Infobase Publishing

Career Launcher: **Computers and Programming**

Copyright © 2010 by Infobase Publishing, Inc.

Ferguson
An imprint of Infobase Publishing
132 West 31st Street
New York NY 10001

Library of Congress Cataloging-in-Publication Data

McCoy, Lisa.
    Computers and programming / Lisa McCoy.
       p. cm. — (Career launcher)
    Includes bibliographical references and index.
    ISBN-13: 978-0-8160-7950-6 (hardcover : alk. paper)
    ISBN-10: 0-8160-7950-1 (hardcover : alk. paper)
1. Computer science—Vocational guidance. I. Title.
    QA76.25.M45 2010
    004.023—dc22

                        2009021393

Ferguson books are available at special discounts when purchased in bulk quantities for businesses, associations, institutions, or sales promotions. Please call our Special Sales Department in New York at (212) 967-8800 or (800) 322-8755.

You can find Ferguson on the World Wide Web at http://www.fergpubco.com

Produced by Print Matters, Inc.
Text design by A Good Thing, Inc.
Cover design by Takeshi Takahashi
Cover printed by Art Print, Taylor, PA
Book printed and bound by Maple Press, York, PA
Date printed: June 2010

Printed in the United States of America

10 9 8 7 6 5 4 3 2 1

This book is printed on acid-free paper.

Contents

Foreword / vii

Acknowledgments / xiii

Introduction / xv

1
Industry History / 1

2
State of the Industry / 26

3
On the Job / 54

4
Tips for Success / 83

5
Talk Like a Pro / 109

6
Resources / 125

Index / 141

Foreword

Congratulations! With *Career Launcher: Computers and Programming* in hand, you are in a great position to effectively manage your new career, which will reward you with more opportunities and enable you to increase your earning potential.

Many of us, me included, took a haphazard approach to career management by choosing jobs for the paycheck rather than the work satisfaction or potential career growth. One of the most costly mistakes you can make is not taking a proactive and informed approach in managing your career. While education, experience, and technical skills may qualify you for a position, your ability to build a productive career path also falls under the scrutiny of potential employers.

Cardiac Science's (http://www.cardiacscience.com) technology focuses on cardiac stress testing equipment, rehabilitation, automated external defibrillators (AEDs), and data management systems. At the base of all the products are computers. Their competitors are Philips and Siemens, so they are up against the big boys and have to stay on the cutting edge or lose market share. They employed programmers, developers, technical project managers, and testers. In my nearly five years with the company, I hired well over 300 people, and 50 percent of my hires were computer professionals.

We had more than 100 employees in three states in technology—both software and hardware. We always had open staffing requisitions for these folks, and they were always hard to find—especially good people with at least four years of experience. That is the most in-demand experience level.

After hiring hundreds of technical people throughout my career, I realized that the most successful candidates had similar philosophies about how they managed and approached their careers. These candidates understand that there are many doors open to them with their technical skills and they make smart choices in order to maximize their potential. Here are some of the commonalities I observed:

The Only Way to Do Great Work Is to Love What You Do.

Steve Jobs, the co-founder and CEO of Apple, wrote this in his 2005 commencement speech to Stanford University graduates. Love what you do and do what you love. Many of us have heard that before. Life is too short to have a job or career that you don't absolutely love doing on a daily basis. When you feel passionate about what you do, you have a greater chance for achievements and success. The sad thing is that so many people are unhappy at their jobs. Many think of it as means to an end—keeping a roof over their heads, making a car payment, and paying their bills. You spend the majority of your waking hours at work and you should enjoy what you do. If you are not sure what you love to do, but you know it involves technology, then stay open to all opportunities and take risks that may lead you to a job or career that you will feel passionate about.

Make Sure You and Your Company Are Compatible. Research companies thoroughly before you interview. Although technical innovation, financial position, and long-term viability are important company attributes, so is culture. Decide what is important to you. Do you want to work for a large company with extensive training and resources, or a smaller company where you are able to see your impact on a daily basis? What kind of corporate culture are you looking for? High performance and fast paced? Collaborative and humanistic? Each organization has its own personality. You will be most successful in a company that exhibits the behaviors that you value.

Your First Job in this Field May Not Be Perfect. It is a stepping stone. Even if you aren't exactly doing what you studied, don't get discouraged. Think about how this job will help you get your next job. What skill set or experience can you acquire that will enrich your resume and make you a strong candidate for your next role? When I graduated in 1990, the economy was in a recession. I landed a job two weeks after graduation because I was willing to take a risk, while my classmates interviewed for months without finding a job. It was not my dream job and the money was not enticing, but I learned a lot and worked with smart people. Be open to all possibilities as the economy will always have its ups and downs. The good news is that despite these challenges, hiring still occurs and smart job seekers can still find employment. All good companies are looking for the same thing: smart, innovative, hard working, and collaborative people.

Climbing the Corporate Ladder May Not Be All It Is Cracked Up to Be. Many people think the road to success leads to management. They work hard, gain leadership skills, and are promoted in to management only to find that they are miserable. If leading a team of people or even managing one person is not your passion, it does not mean that you have decreased your earning potential and professional status. I have worked with numerous high-level technical managers who have made a conscientious choice to return to an individual contributor role and have found much more contentment in their work.

Find a Mentor. A good mentor asks you great questions, challenges your assumptions, and often open doors for you. You want to choose someone who is already successful in your field. They have been down the path you are entering and have learned how to navigate it successfully. Take the opportunity to observe their work habits and their approach to problem solving. Utilize them for coaching you through work and career issues and challenging you to think at a higher level professionally.

Network, Network, Network. Networking is not as complicated as you might think. Take every opportunity to meet new people who share your professional interests. Join a professional organization in your field and keep in touch with your alumni association. Today, most jobs are found through networking rather than traditional methods such as online job boards and company websites. Start creating a professional online presence. Set up a profile on LinkedIn, the leading online professional network and start linking to professionals you know—your friends and family members, alumni, and former co-workers. One caution, be careful what you communicate on MySpace, Facebook, and blogs, as employers often search those sites when they are recruiting you. You don't want to post any disparaging information that may prevent you from being considered for a position.

Antisocial Geeks Are Out. You are more than just a technical professional. Gone are the days when strong technical skills overcame a shortage of people or social skills. You will need to develop more than just the left side of your brain. Successful people in the technology field can write, speak, and relate to all levels within the organization. You may be most comfortable in front of a computer screen but you will also need to be able to effectively communicate throughout the organization. Having this ability opens doors to higher level opportunities where your communication skills are essential to your success in those roles.

Learn Continually. Education is essential as you start your career and will allow you to have as many opportunities as possible available to you. Bachelors of science in engineering, computer science, information sciences, mathematics, or related fields are among the degrees employers in this field are often looking for. I have also seen people entering this field who have business degrees and have taken programming courses.

Internships are a great way to gain experience while in school and will give you an edge over other entry-level programmers who have only educational experience. To stay competitive in the job market, computer programmers should continue to learn new languages and keep up with new developments and trends.

Each company will want programming experience specific to their technology. Some of the top languages used today are Java, C, C++, C#, Perl, JavaScript, Visual Basic .Net, PHP, Ajax, Python and Ruby.

More and more programmers work on and oversee large projects. Project management experience is a great way to distinguish yourself from others and often leads to more of a leadership role.

Technology is constantly evolving and you need to continue to hone and expand your skills throughout your career. Keep abreast of changes in the industry and respond accordingly. Understand that you have more opportunities when your skills sets are current and marketable.

Exit Gracefully. If you leave your job for a better opportunity or if you realize it is not a great fit, you always want to leave on good terms. Give your employer proper notice, especially if you are in the middle of a project. If you are not happy with your current job, let your manager know and discuss the possibility of other opportunities that may be available within the company. If you find that your company is not able to offer the right opportunity for you, understand that not every work place can meet every individual need. The key is to always treat people with respect and professionalism so that you build relationships and references instead of burning bridges. Future employers look at how you treat your former employers as an indicator of how you would treat them.

Being Fired May Be a Blessing. It is definitely not the end of the world, but a signal to you that you need to focus on a new opportunity. Most people will experience being fired at some point in their career. Steve Jobs was fired after being at Apple for 10 years and building it into a $2 billion dollar business. What could be worse than being fired from a company that you co-founded? For him it was freeing and helped him put his energies into a new direction that eventually led him to co-found Pixar Animation Studios. If you find yourself in this predicament—warranted or not—know that it is freeing you for a better opportunity. Be open with future employers about your termination. You never want to make disparaging remarks about your former employer, but do express that there was a parting of the ways. If they want further detail, be very brief and professional in how you explain the circumstances.

Plan for Success. This book will give you an amazing glimpse into the computer and programming industry, with its forward-looking and historical perspectives. Understanding the industry you are entering and the ability to successfully navigate through your field of work gives you the advantage over your competition. Utilize this book as a resource to plan, develop, evolve, and thrive in your career. Good luck!

Vicki Campbell
DIRECTOR, HUMAN RESOURCES
GACO WESTERN, LLC

Acknowledgments

The author would like to gratefully acknowledge the following people for their repeated willingness to share their experience and insights—their help was truly invaluable:

Vicki Campbell, Roberta Croly, Ramon Infante, Dean Katona, Patrick Maninger, Ed McKillop, Anne Moss, Rob Short, Bill Weis, and Darcey Woodard.

Introduction

Perhaps when you think of careers involving computers, you think of the quintessential "geek" writing code. While some in the field encourage and embrace that stereotype, the field of computers and computer programming encompasses so much more. The type of work a person in this field may do is wide-ranging. There are software developers, computer technicians, and hardware developers, to be sure; however, careers in the computer industry can also be had in the areas of medicine, film, gaming, law enforcement, and more. Practically no business exists today that doesn't use computer technology in some form—whether it's a system for tracking inventory and processing customer orders, scanning the price of items in a grocery store, or running a diagnostic test on a car.

Computers are ubiquitous and pervasive, touching almost every aspect of our lives. Consider what you did today. Perhaps you withdrew money from an ATM. Maybe you downloaded files to work on at home. You may have participated in a meeting in which some people were in Seattle, some in Arizona, and some in New York, yet everyone was "together" in the same virtual location and able to see the same video presentation. You likely checked your e-mail—maybe several times. Perhaps your phone or television service—or both—are made possible by an Internet service provider. You could even be reading this book on an electronic device rather than in bound form. No matter what you did, it is likely that computer science and technology had a hand in those tasks. Some people do not even know a world without computers, the Internet, e-mail, iPods, and so on. The majority of kids today do not know a world without Google. It is easy to take this technology for granted.

Career Launchers: Computers and Programming will teach you everything you need to know about this exciting—and vast—industry. It is designed for people who are entering the computer industry and will provide everything you need to know to succeed in this field, from basic concepts and terminology, to information about current "hot" areas and possible future trends, to statistics on employment and what to do to advance your career.

This book is divided into six chapters. You can read the book in its entirety, or jump to the chapters that provide the information you need at the moment. Chapter 1 provides a snapshot history of the industry, from its beginnings to the present. This chapter is designed to acquaint readers with the full scope of the computing industry— its origins, noteworthy figures in its history, where it's been, where it's going, and what drives it today. A brief chronology of this industry is also provided. Established professionals will help you understand how the industry's past is shaping its future.

Once you have a general idea of the history behind computing, Chapter 2 provides a detailed overview of the current state of the industry. Information is included on typical salaries for programmers, database administrators, Web site designers, and others, with a breakdown according to industry. For example, a software programmer working for a publisher made $79,270 a year in 2006, whereas a programmer working for an insurance carrier made $65,650 that same year. You will learn about the major players—companies like Microsoft, Google, and IBM—and how it feels to work for a larger company versus working for a smaller one. Statistics are included with regard to company profits, number of employees, and the unique role these companies play in shaping the industry. Future trends in computing are also examined, such as green IT, artificial intelligence, and social networking. In addition, some of the key conferences and industry events are described. Participation in these can help move a computing career forward. Not only is there knowledge to be gained, but there are connections to be made... connections that may put you in touch with just the right person to help you advance your career. This chapter ends with an exploration of the presence of women in this industry. Largely thought of as a male-dominated field, this trend is starting to change, and the size of the company a woman works for may have something to do with it. Building on this information about the computer industry as a whole—its history, its current state, and its possible future—Chapter 3 provides a detailed, alphabetical listing of key jobs and positions within this industry and how they coordinate with each other. It's a glossary of sorts, defining the roles of people in different departments that are common to most companies in the industry, regardless of size. Understanding the links between positions and levels can reveal paths to career advancement, so this chapter will describe how skill sets for certain positions can overlap and lead to promotion. For example, in a small company, a person who is great at network administration might also be great at understanding phone systems—and vice versa. Of course, every individual is different and career paths can vary widely—people often start in one area and end up in a different one than they had envisioned. This chapter will provide guidelines so that people new to the computing industry understand not only their position, but also other positions and the roles everyone plays to keep the business moving. This knowledge, in turn, can help when planning the possible directions of a career in this industry.

Chapter 4 provides a wealth of information on how to thrive and succeed in this industry. Everyone likely knows the importance of not lying on your resume, conducting themselves in a professional manner, the basics of interviewing, and so on, but, more specifically, how is success in the computing industry achieved? This chapter provides the do's and don'ts you need to know to move up the ladder and how to approach your career to best move it forward. Whether you work at a large company or a small one, established professionals tell you how to get ahead. How do you find a mentor (and when is that a drawback)? How important is a degree versus certification? Is certification even important? How much does experience count? Are some degrees looked on more favorably than others? This chapter also compares working for a large company with working at a small one—for example, people at smaller companies are often expected to wear many different hats, whereas people at larger companies may have to find a niche area and specialize. Tips on how to establish a professional reputation—and mistakes that can ruin it—are also included.

Chapter 5 offers an in-depth guide to industry jargon, key terminology, industry-specific phrases and concepts, and general business terms. Practically every field has terminology that is specific to it, and computing is no exception. (In fact, it can be argued that it's more jargon-laden than many other industries!) After reading this chapter, you will know how to talk like a pro—just remember the importance of reining in the temptation to use jargon and technical terms with "non-techies."

While this book covers different aspects of launching a successful career in computers and programming, it cannot possibly cover everything. Chapter 6 fills in the gaps by pointing you to key publications, Web sites, books, schools, and training programs that are relevant to anyone working in the industry today. Subscribing to certain periodicals and journals, for example, or joining trade organizations and associations relevant to your specific position can provide the edge needed to push a career forward. Those who stay abreast of developments in this field move forward; those who do not quickly get left behind.

Throughout each chapter, you will find the following boxed items, which contain information that supplements each chapter:

Best Practices: These will tell you how to improve your efficiency and performance in the workplace. Some are aimed at the computing industry; others apply to a person's career in general.

Everyone Knows: These items provide essential information that everyone in the computing industry should know. This information is crucial. Not knowing these things might even cost you a job!

Fast Facts: On the other hand, if you want to impress someone in your next interview, you might toss out one of these handy tidbits of information. These items provide fun, useful bits of information that, while not necessary knowledge, may make you look good.

Keeping In Touch: Even if you embrace the label "computer geek," it doesn't mean you have to act like one. These items will provide tips for effective business communication—through e-mail, on the phone, and in person—and include pointers on maintaining professionalism at all times. Effective networking tips are also included.

On the Cutting Edge: These items discuss emerging trends and state-of-the-art technology in this industry. You may find these items helpful when considering a specialty or looking toward the future of your computing career.

Problem Solving: While this book can't possibly cover every contingency, it can describe common, hypothetical problems often encountered by people in this industry and offer possible solutions.

Professional Ethics: Just as professionalism is important—regardless of the career you are in or how lax your boss is—so are strong ethics. These items describe an ethical dilemma and its successful resolution, with an emphasis on how ethical conduct can help build a strong career.

Clearly, a career in computers and programming can mean much more than typing code. While your degree may be in computer science, information technology, or a related area, you may find yourself working in banking, medicine, defense technologies, gaming, healthcare, forensics—the possibilities are endless. This book will serve as a companion on your career path and offer you the tips, tools, and knowledge that can help you succeed. Once you've launched your career, where you take it is entirely up to you.

Chapter 1

Industry History

What is a computer? Today, the answer ranges from the iconic desktop computer to a phone, a car's navigation system, a blood sugar monitor, and everything in between. Computers are ubiquitous; they are a pervasive part of nearly every aspect of our lives. A 2005 survey by the Kaiser Family Foundation revealed that 31 percent of children in the United States have a computer in their room (up from 21 percent the year before). From 1999 to 2004, the proportion of U.S. homes that have two or more computers jumped from 25 percent to 39 percent, and the proportion with Internet access in the home grew from 47 percent to 74 percent. The percentage of children who can surf the Web from the privacy of their own bedroom doubled from 10 percent to 20 percent. These statistics are amazing when you consider that computers didn't truly emerge as a force—at least not from a consumer standpoint—until the 1950s.

Make no mistake—it's a hot industry to work in today—and likely to remain so in the future. Consider the following areas in which computers play a role: computer-assisted conceptualization, computer-assisted learning, automatic translation, musical composition, graphic design, computer animation, prosthetics, robotics... whatever job you can think of, computers likely play a role.

When the term "computer" was coined in 1646 (perhaps earlier), it referred to humans who performed calculations. The *Oxford English Dictionary, Second Edition*, dates the use of the word "computer" as referring to a mechanical calculating device to 1897 in the January 22 issue of the journal *Engineering*. Today, according to *Webster's Third*

International Dictionary, a computer is defined as "a programmable electronic device that can store, retrieve, and process data." These devices—be they an ATM machine, a scanner in a grocery store, or components of the Space Shuttle—all perform calculations, ranging from simple to complex, that help us in our day-to-day lives. We often are not aware of these calculations, but when computers fail to do their job, the vital roles that they play in modern life are revealed to us. For example, from August 2008 to January 2009, computer glitches in the display of health records at Veterans' Administration (VA) hospitals caused some patients to be given incorrect doses of drugs or to have treatments delayed. Fortunately, no one appeared to be seriously harmed or killed as a result of the glitches, but the potential was there. In 2008, a sudden drop in altitude of Qantas Flight 72 over Western Australia was due to a computer error. While the pilots were able to recover from the two sudden, severe drops in altitude, eleven passengers on the flight were seriously injured.

How It All Began

The history of computing can go all the way back to the abacus—once humans started counting things, "computing" began. However, a full treatment of this history is beyond the scope of this book. This chapter focuses on the modern history of the computer, focusing mostly on the early 20th century, with some earlier background where relevant. Recounting the lives and achievements of every single notable person involved would take an entire book—and indeed many books have been devoted to this topic. Readers interested in learning more about the history of computing should consult chapter 6.

The history of the computer is complex, involving a myriad of players and taking place in several different countries at once, including the United States, England, and Japan. It is not possible to trace it in a linear fashion; rather, it is more like a cluster diagram—ideas developing in tandem and people building on each other's ideas, a long succession of responses to perceived needs. No single person deserves credit for inventing the computer. As John Atanasoff—widely considered the "father of the computer"—put it, "There is enough credit for everyone in the invention and development of the electronic computer."

However, some names have come to the forefront and certain aspects of computing technology—such as Aiken, UNIVAC, and IBM—are more well known than others because they surpassed their technologically inferior brethren that fell by the wayside: the

Best Practice

In early 2009, more than 30 U.S. and international cybersecurity organizations released a list of the 25 leading programming errors that affect security on the Web. According to the SANS (SysAdmin, Audit, Network, Security) Institute, these errors are serious: "Two of the errors alone led to more than 1.5 million Web site security breaches during 2008, and the effect of those breaches was multiplied because malware on the tainted Web sites turned the computers of visitors into zombies [a computer that a remote attacker has accessed and set up to forward transmissions (including spam and viruses) to other computers on the Internet]." These errors fall into one of three categories:

Insecure interaction between computers: Examples include failure to preserve the structure of a Web page, improper input validation, and cross-site request forgery.

Risky resource management: Examples include improper resource shutdown or release, downloading code without an integrity check, and incorrect calculations.

Porous defenses: Examples include improper access control, use of insufficiently random values, and client-side enforcement of server-side security.

For the complete list of these errors, with in-depth information on their impact, their importance, and resources for detecting and repairing them, visit http://www.sans.org/top25errors.

punchcard, the vacuum tube circuit, and Apple's Lisa, for example. The sections that follow highlight a few of the noteworthy names and explain their role in the development of the modern computer. Some readers will note that certain names are missing from this history. This omission is intentional. Again, chapter 6 will point readers to more comprehensive and in-depth information.

The Players and the Pieces

While computers have led to some entertaining applications—computer and video games immediately come to mind—their development was driven by the need to conduct calculations faster and more accurately than previous technology. According to Georges Ifrah, a professor of mathematics and author of *The Universal History of Numbers* and *The Universal History of Computing*, "Calculation is slow, tedious, and above all tedious...and this has given rise to all sorts of hindrances...this is why scientists have always sought to simplify their various calculations." Initially, military and business needs drove the computer's development and then consumer applications followed. Today, some argue that it is the other way around—that the consumer now drives advances in the computing industry, a point that will be elaborated on throughout this book.

The Genesis of Computers

The early "computers" as they are thought of today—really just glorified adding machines—were mechanical in nature. They did not run on electricity (that concept was hundreds of years away) and consisted of primitive gears and wheels and other mechanical parts. In 1642, the French philosopher and mathematician Blaise Pascal devised an adding machine to help his father, a tax collector. This "calculator" used a series of ten-toothed wheels; each tooth represented a digit from 0 to 9. The wheels were connected so that numbers could be added to each other by advancing the wheels by a correct number of teeth. A train of eight moveable dials could be used to add numbers up to eight digits long. As a dial turned one full turn of numbers 1 through 10, the dial automatically turned the next dial. This machine was limited, however, in that it could only be used for addition and subtraction.

Pascal's adding machine can be considered a precursor to the modern computer, and the machine—and its potential—certainly were not forgotten. In the 1670s, the German philosopher and mathematician Gottfried Wilhelm von Leibniz improved on Pascal's "arithmetic machine" by inventing one that could multiply as well. Leibniz, however, took Pascal's machine yet another step further. He saw how it could be altered to use a binary system of calculation, which is what computers today operate on. Briefly, the term "binary" refers to a dual system of calculation whereby values are expressed in one of two states, represented by either a 1 or a 0. This concept is at the heart of digital computing, a concept that will be expanded upon shortly.

During the late 1790s, Joseph-Marie Jacquard, a French straw hat maker and silk weaver turned inventor, was working on a loom that could weave complicated patterns described by holes in punched cards. While it did not compute anything, this mechanical loom has a place in the history of computing because its ability to change the pattern of the loom's weave simply by changing cards was an important concept in the development of computer programming. In fact, Charles Babbage, an English mathematician, philosopher, inventor, and mechanical engineer, used a similar concept in creating his "analytical engine." The analytical engine could be programmed using punched cards that were more complex than Jacquard's, consisting of stiff paper that stored bits of information in columns containing patterns of punched holes. Babbage realized that if a person programmed a set of "instructions" by way of these punched cards, they could be put in the machine and the machine could carry out the instructions automatically.

The difference engine was an automatic mechanical calculator that was never completed but is still considered one of the first general-purpose digital computers. Babbage designed it to calculate various mathematical functions, including trigonometric and logarithmic functions.

Today, computers are digital, but they began as analog machines. An analog computer measures data that varies continuously in value, such as temperature, sound, frequency, or pressure. Analog computers are used to create data models in order to solve a specific problem. And therein lies their weakness. Analog computers must be built for a specific purpose. Digital computers are what most people think of when they hear the word "computer." A digital computer operates most often using a binary system in which two different states—"on" and "off"—are used to represent all types of information, from numbers to letters to symbols to program instructions.

The 20th Century

In the first half of the 20th century, work on calculating machines continued. In 1919, E.O. Carissan, a lieutenant in the French infantry, designed and built a mechanical device for factoring positive or negative whole numbers (called integers) and testing whether they were a prime number. (A prime number is a positive number that only has two divisors: the number itself and 1.) In 1910, Leonardo Torres y Quevedo, a Spanish engineer and mathematician built several electromechanical calculating devices, including one that played simple chess endgames.

In 1936, Alan Turing, a British mathematician, logician and cryptanalyst, and Alonzo Church, an American mathematician and logician, introduced the formalization of an algorithm, with limits on what can be computed, and a "purely mechanical" model for computing. Known as the Church-Turing thesis, this hypothesis about the nature of mechanical calculation devices, such as electronic computers, claims that any calculation that is possible can be performed by an algorithm running on a computer, provided that sufficient time and storage space are available. The Turing machine, which was developed in tandem with the thesis, has an infinitely long tape and a read/write head (read/write refers to the ability to both read and make changes to a piece of data) that can move along the tape, changing the values along the way. While the machine is obviously an impossibility—something that can only exist in theory—it can simulate the computation of any algorithm that can be performed on a modern computer.

Fast Facts

Howard Aiken, inventor of the Mark I, never believed that a commercial market could exist for the computer. In 1948, he believed that perhaps five or six computers would be needed in the United States, but no more than that. How wrong he was! According to the analyst firm Forrester, PC numbers worldwide are predicted to hit 2 billion by 2015, with more than 1 billion in use by the end of 2008.

Howard Aiken and the Mark I

Howard Aiken was an inventor and professor of applied mathematics at Harvard. With the help of colleagues at Massachusetts Institute of Technology (MIT), Harvard, and International Business Machines (IBM), Aiken invented the Mark I during the early 1940s. It performed calculations using a combination of electrical and mechanical components and relays (an electrical switch that opens and closes based on another electrical switch), and is considered the first large-scale automatic digital computer. The instruction sequence used to solve a problem—the program—was fed into the machine on a roll of punched paper tape, rather than being stored in the computer.

In 1945, the idea of storing the program within the computer was introduced, based on the concepts of mathematician John von Neumann. The instructions would be stored within a "memory," freeing the computer from the speed limitations of the paper tape reader during execution and permitting problems to be solved without rewiring the computer.

John Atanasoff and ABC

John Atanasoff, a professor from Iowa State College, first conceived of the idea of an electronic digital computer in 1930 (the Mark I relied on mechanical and electronic components). The device consisted of a rotating drum on which 1,600 capacitors (pairs of conductors separated by a nonconducting substance) were placed in 32 rows. Each capacitor could be charged positively, indicating a 1, or negatively, indicating a 0. Today's computers operate on the same binary principle.

In the early 1940s, the completed version, the Atanasoff Berry Computer (ABC) was finished. According to Mike Hally, the author of *Electronic Brains: Stories from the Dawn of the Computer Age*, it was "as big as a fridge, weighed a third of a ton, and used more than 300 tubes...and it took 15 seconds to complete an arithmetic calculation." The device was designed to resolve systems of linear equations, but it was rudimentary, not programmable, and didn't always work properly.

John Mauchly, Presper Eckert, and ENIAC

During the 1880s, the American statistician Herman Hollerith devised a system that passed punched cards over electrical contacts. His machine enabled both the counting and sorting of data—a significant milestone in the computer's development. As a result, Hollerith's machine was used to compile statistical information for the 1890 U.S. census. The U.S. Census Bureau, however, quickly outgrew this punchcard system. In 1950, two men—John Mauchly and Presper Eckert—stepped up to fill this need.

John Mauchly, a mathematician and physicist, and Presper Eckert, an electrical engineer, wanted to do something bigger and better than what Atanasoff had done. Their goal was to produce a computer that could perform calculations in 10 minutes or less. Thus began work on the Electronic Numerical Integrator and Computer, or ENIAC.

ENIAC is considered the predecessor of most computers in use today. According to Paul Ceruzzi, the author of *A History of Modern*

Computing, its purpose was to calculate firing tables for the U.S. Army. (A firing table contains artillery settings, based on both test firings and computer simulations, given a certain set of conditions.) This task "involved the repetitive solution of complex mathematical expressions, [and ENIAC] occupied a room that was 50 feet by 30 feet, contained 18,000 tubes and 70,000 resistors," and was much like the clichéd image that comes to mind when one thinks of the first computers.

Aiken was a rival of Mauchly and Eckert, and was often dismissive of their work. In fact, he was part of a committee that recommended the U.S. National Bureau of Standards not support Eckert and Mauchly's work, calling their proposal "foolishness."

UNIVAC

The next venture for Mauchly and Eckert was one they wanted to see used for military, business, and scientific purposes, so they called it the Universal Automatic Computer (UNIVAC). Between financial setbacks, World War II, and Senator Joseph McCarthy's war on Communism at home, it looked like the UNIVAC would never get off the ground. The U.S. government, however, was very interested in Mauchly and Eckert's new project. In 1950, the U.S. Census Bureau needed a new way to calculate results. Up to this point, results were manually counted. However, this process was too slow to keep up with population growth and the results were taking too long to process. UNIVAC was the answer to their dilemma.

Developments in Hardware: From Room Size to Pocket Size

In the late 1950s, transistors (components used to amplify a signal) were employed in computers, which led to smaller, faster, and more versatile components than were possible with vacuum-tube machines like the ENIAC. The first commercial computer to use transistors was developed in 1957 by Seymour R. Cray, a pioneer in the design of supercomputers. Because transistors use less power than vacuum tubes and have a longer life, this development alone was responsible for the improved machines called *second-generation computers*, the first generation being those that employed vacuum tubes. Components became smaller, as did the spacings between components, and systems became much less expensive to build.

Smaller, Faster, and Less Expensive

By the 1950s, the idea of the "personal" computer was starting to take form and the realization was dawning that there was indeed a market for these amazing machines—provided the user interface could be improved upon.

The 1960s saw improvements to the computer's user interface. Both private and government-funded research projects were everywhere: MIT, the Information Processing Techniques Office, Advanced Research Projects Agency (ARPA), Dartmouth College, and Stanford Research Institute, among others. These projects led to the development of the mouse, computer networks, the BASIC (Beginner's All-purpose Symbolic Instruction Code) programming language, and the concept of time sharing, among other things. (Time sharing, in this context, refers to sharing computer resources through multitasking.)

There was still no personal computer, per se. Rather, most computers were large mainframes shared by several users. Microcomputers were beginning to appear for scientific and commercial use. The cost decreased from $85,000 in 1961 to $8,500 in 1967. However, they were still only available to technical and professional users. In 1966, Hewlett-Packard (HP) released one of the first microcomputers, the Model 2116, followed by the 2114A, which sold for $9,950.

Hobbyists were a driving force in the development of the personal computer. These amateurs were devoted—it wasn't easy, or cheap, to build a computer—and had an extensive knowledge of vacuum tubes, transistor circuitry, digital logic, core memory, peripherals, and more. In January 1968, hobbyists' computers had an average clock rate of 500 kilohertz and a memory ranging from 4 to 8 kilobytes in size. Most used discrete transistors; a few used integrated circuits (miniature electronic circuits). Machines using integrated circuits are considered the third generation of computers. The most common input/output device was a Teletype terminal, which is a basically an electromechanical typewriter. The average cost was $650.

According to Roy Allan, the author of *A History of the Personal Computer*, the creation of the transistor in 1947 and the development of the integrated circuit in 1959 formed the basis for the microprocessor. By the late 1960s, chips with thousands of components were available. And they were about to get even better.

In general, computers in the 1970s were able to check eight binary digits, or bits, of data, at every cycle or switch. (A switch is an electrical component that can break an electrical circuit, interrupting the current or diverting it from one conductor to another.) A group of eight bits is called a byte, and each byte contains 256 possible patterns of ones and zeros. Each pattern is the equivalent of an instruction, a part of an instruction, or a piece of data.

In 1971, the Intel Corporation was born. It began life as NM Electronics, named after its founders, Robert Noyce and Gordon Moore. The initial focus of Intel was to develop a large-scale integrated memory chip to replace magnetic core memory, an early form of random access memory. In 1970, Intel introduced the 1103 chip, the world's first 1 kilobyte dynamic random access memory (RAM) chip. In 1971, the Intel 4044 chip became commercially available. Integrating four chips, it sold for $2,000. Companies like Texas Instruments, Motorola, MOS Technology, Zolig, and Hewlett-Packard introduced microprocessors of their own. The 8-bit and then 16-bit processors were introduced, followed by processors that can handle 16, 32, and 64 bits of data at a time, increasing the speed of computers. Thus, the fourth generation of computers—those based on the microprocessor—was born. The total list of operations that a computer is capable of is called its instruction set. Both the number of bits that can be processed at a time and the size of instruction sets continue to increase.

The Personal Computer and the Consumer Market

The definition of *personal computer* was changing as well. *Personal* was now coming to mean that the average person could afford to own one. This became possible by a change in not just the software, but in the hardware as well. The microprocessor and the memory chip replaced discrete components and core memory. As a result, computers were less complicated and less expensive. According to Roy Allan, "factory-built 'turn-key' units changed the market from the computer hobbyist and software enthusiast to the 'appliance user' and a larger consumer market."

This newly expanding market for personal computers attracted all sorts of companies. In October 1970, IBM announced the System/3 Model 6. This disk-based system featured a BASIC user interface. However, on average, the system cost $48,250, so it was largely excluded from the consumer market. In 1971, the Kenbak Corporation released the Kenbak-1, among the first commercially assembled, low-cost personal computers, for around $750. In 1972, HP released a low-cost, 16-bit, general-purpose computer, the HP 3000 minicomputer.

In 1970, the Xerox Corporation, largely (and still) known for its copiers, decided that it, too, wanted to enter the general computer market. Xerox founded the Palo Alto Research Center (PARC) in northern California and acquired Scientific Data Systems, a company that had been manufacturing computers for the engineering and scientific fields. First to emerge from PARC was the Alto: It consisted of a processor, disk storage cabinet, bit-mapped graphics display, keyboard, and mouse. It had a 16-bit CPU and sold for an estimated $20,000 to $32,000. Other innovations that came out of PARC include the graphical user interface (which used icons and other visual indicators to represent the information and actions available to a user), overlapping windows, pop-up menus, icons, a WYSIWYG (what you see is what you get) word-processing program, the object-oriented language called SmallTalk, and the use of an Ethernet network to connect computers and peripherals.

Everyone Knows

At its heart, a bit is a single piece of information corresponding to either one of two values, represented as either 0 or 1. It is a basic unit of information storage and communication. According to Roy Allan, author of *A History of the Personal Computer: The People and the Technology*, the first documented use of the term was in an internal memo by John W. Tuckey at the AT&T Bell Laboratories in 1947.

A byte is an ordered collection of bits (usually 8 bits, but this can vary). The first documented use of this term, according to Allan, was in regard to the development of the IBM Stretch Computer in a 1956 internal memo.

The concept of combining hardware and software to come up with a friendly user interface was unique. Apple and Microsoft would take these concepts and build on this technology when designing their microcomputers. Windows, anyone?

By the time the 1980s arrived, some companies were falling by the wayside and others were snatching them up. For example, Intel and Advanced Micro Devices (AMD) entered into a ten-year exchange agreement (Intel was losing market share to Motorola and had to do something), IBM purchased first 12 percent and then 20 percent of Intel, Exxon acquired Zolig and then sold it back to Zolig executives, and AT&T bought Synterek, a Honeywell division.

In 1981, Intel produced a 32-bit microprocessor with an advanced design that improved data storage capabilities. Also in 1981, IBM made a significant impact on the PC market with the release of its IBM Personal Computer. An aggressive price war resulted among companies, causing financial problems for many. A few, however, managed to survive the competition.

Tandy/Radio Shack, for example, had introduced the TRS-80 Model III computer in 1980. The computer included 4 kilobytes of expandable RAM, a non-detachable keyboard, and a high-resolution 12-inch monitor. Three different configurations were available, ranging in price from $699 to $2,485. Additional products followed, decreasing in size and cost and increasing in capabilities and features.

Commodore International released the Commodore 64 in January 1982. According to Leander Kahney, author of *Inside Steve's Brain* and *The Cult of Mac*, during the Commodore 64's lifetime, sales totaled 30 million units, making it the best-selling single personal computer model of all time. Part of the Commodore 64's success was because it was sold in retail stores instead of electronics stores. Commodore also produced many of its parts in-house to control supplies and cost. The basic configuration had 20 kilobytes of read-only memory (ROM) and 64 kilobytes of RAM. Upon its release, the Commodore 64 sold for $595, but by 1983, the price had dropped to less than $400.

Other notable companies competing at this time include Osborne, Kaypro, and Compaq. Compaq was founded in 1982. The name, a play on the word *compact*, was designed to reflect the founders' idea of what would make Compaq computers unique. Compaq was the first company to successfully compete with IBM by providing a similar computer—a feat they achieved by reverse-engineering the IBM ROM BIOS chip. Later in 1982, Compaq released the Compaq Portable. It had 128 kilobytes of RAM, which could be expanded to 256 kilobytes, and a 320 kilobyte double-sided floppy disk built in. This computer was 20 inches wide by 8.5 inches high and weighed 28 pounds. A basic one-disk system cost $2,995, and a two-disk system cost $3,590.

Another notable competitor still in existence today is Dell. As a teenager, Michael S. Dell started buying, upgrading, and selling

IBM-compatible computers. This was the beginning of Dell's business model: bypassing the intermediary and selling computers directly to the end user. This approach eliminated the markup to dealers and resellers, and provided a significant cost advantage when it came to product pricing. In 1986, Dell introduced the fastest-performing personal computer system available at that time. With a speed of 12 megahertz and a price of $1,995, it was superior to IBM's 6 megahertz model, which sold for $3,995. By the end of 1986, Dell had sales of about $60 million.

Sun Microsystems, Inc., while not known for its personal computers, is known for its engineering and scientific workstations. Founded in 1982, the company's primary goal was to produce a low-cost, general-purpose computer that could be connected to a network. The result—the Sun-3 series of workstations—was highly successful and led to their slogan, "The network is the computer."

How Fast Is Fast?

As computers became smaller and more mainstream, the speed with which they could carry out their tasks improved as well. Everything a computer does is based on one thing: determining if a switch, or "gate," is open or closed (often signaled using the numbers 0 and 1). This is the essence of the binary system that underlies all of modern computing, and it is the speed at which computers perform this simple act that makes them so amazing.

A key factor in a computer's speed is its clock—a timing device that sends rapid pulses to the components to synchronize and pace them. Essentially, the faster the clock, the more operations per second the computer will perform. A computer's speed and calculating power are further enhanced by the amount of data handled during each cycle. For example, if a computer checks only one switch at a time, that switch can represent only two commands or numbers; thus ON would symbolize one operation or number, and OFF would symbolize another. By checking groups of switches linked as a unit, however, the computer increases the number of operations it can recognize at each cycle.

Other techniques can be used to increase computer speed. A cache is a small section of memory that stores recently used data on the assumption that the data may need to be accessed again in the near future. Having the data nearby thus reduces the time required to access it. In addition, multiprocessing, or parallel processing, boosts speed by performing many operations simultaneously on two or more chips. As many as a thousand microprocessor chips work together in massively parallel processing.

The Role of the Keyboard

Without the invention of the keyboard, computers might never have become the superpower they are today. While the early calculation machines, such as those invented by Blaise Pascal, Frank Baldwin, and Charles Xavier-Thomas, were certainly an improvement over manual calculation devices, their performance was still slow when compared to a human. This was because of how the numbers were entered into the machine. According to George Ifrah, "this involved the movement of a slide or lever within a straight or curved slot and required the use of at least two fingers."

In the middle of the 19th century, however, the typewriter influenced the development of the computer keyboard.

The histories of companies like IBM, Intel, Microsoft, and Apple fill volumes; an extensive treatment of those histories is beyond the scope of this book. For resources to find further information about the history of the computer consult chapter 6.

Making Connections: The Development of the Internet

Along with the development of the computer came the idea to enable them to communicate with one another, sharing information and ideas. Not surprisingly, the genesis for this communication began with the military.

ARPANET and the Internet

The Internet as we know it today began life as ARPANET (Advanced Research Projects Agency Network). It uses packet-switching technology (a message delivery technique) and TCP/IP (a communications protocol) to communicate. Technically, the Internet is not a single network; rather, it is a connection of thousands—possibly millions—of networks worldwide. Some of the networks are private—your company's intranet site, for example, or a banking Web site—and others are public—a department store's Web site, for example, or other shopping sites.

In August 1962, J. C. R. Licklider, a computer scientist at MIT, wrote a series of memos detailing a globally interconnected set of computers through which everyone could quickly access data and programs from any site. Always forward-thinking, Licklider recognized several hurdles that would need to be overcome before his vision of a "mechanically extended man" could be realized. Paul Ceruzzi writes: "Some [technical hurdles] involved hardware limits, which existing trends in computer circuits would soon overcome. [Others involved] redefining the notions of programming and data storage as they were then practiced."

Prior to this, in July 1961, Leonard Kleinrock, another computer scientist at MIT, published the first paper on packet-switching theory. Kleinrock believed that packets, or units of information, rather than circuits were the key to computer networking. The other key step was to make the computers talk together. A small experiment, in which a computer in Massachusetts was connected to one in California with a low-speed dial-up telephone line—creating the first wide-area computer network, albeit small—proved that time-shared computers could work well together. They could run programs and retrieve data on the remote computer, but the circuit-switched telephone system (the system in use back then) was inadequate for the job. The need for packet switching was confirmed.

ARPANET was designed to defray the costs of computing resources, which were expensive at that time. (The subsequent invention of the Ethernet—a means of connecting local computer networks—made this factor largely irrelevant.). The mainstream uses of ARPANET quickly became apparent, and it rapidly evolved for commercial use.

On the Cutting Edge

Wash-and-wear computers? While the concept may seem like science fiction, it's closer to becoming a reality than you might think. Eleksen Group PLC, a world leader in what are called "touch-sensitive interactive textiles," has devised a technology called ElekTex. This is a fabric-based, pressure-sensitive control interface that can be integrated into jackets, bags, and other products. At the 2007 Consumer Electronics Show in Las Vegas, Eleksen presented its latest design concept: a laptop carrying case with a display that is integrated with the Windows Vista Slideshow feature. Special devices wirelessly transmit Slideshow content to the display screen, even allowing for remote control and interaction.

INTERVIEW

Hot Areas

Rob Short

Former corporate vice president for Windows core technology, Microsoft

How long have you been in this field? What drew you to it?

I have been in the computer industry for 30 years, having started as a technician in Ireland testing and repairing DEC PDP 11's [a line of personal computers sold by Digital Equipment Corporation from 1970 through the 1990s], moving through various positions in manufacturing and then design and development, and ending as corporate vice president for Windows core technology at Microsoft.

What is the most important thing someone needs to know when entering this field?

This industry is changing much faster than other fields, so it's important to not get tied to an area of technology. It's great to be an expert [in a particular area], but don't be afraid to move on to something else. While the past certainly provides the foundation for the future, interesting innovations occur when there are breaks from the past. Consider the iPod: It's a computer, but that's not how you think about it.

Have you seen the "hot areas" in this industry change over time or have they remained the same? What do you see as "hot areas?"

There is a hot area for every interest: kernels, device drivers, and compilers for the people who love technology, user interface design for [those] who want to change how people actually use computers, and the world of Web applications is so broad it covers almost every interest.

Using computers to advance other fields of study is most interesting for the future. The field is huge—look at image recognition, graphical games, etc. People use physics to model the behavior of objects in games. This was a dream only a few years ago. Now everyone does it. Another trend is the addition of computing power in everyday devices: cell phones receiving e-mail, GPS maps in our cars—even my camera has more computing power and storage than the first computers I worked on.

One thing that's interesting is that even though you can look at technology charts and predict where we'll be in terms of processing power, memory, network bandwidth, etc., it is very hard to really grasp what this means in terms of the capability of the systems [that] can be built. The deep technology should become more invisible to end users even as it enables more powerful and different features.

By 1995, commercial users dominated all other users, such as military, educational, and scientific users.

Initially, users of the Internet could log into a remote computer, transfer files, and send electronic mail. Bulletin board systems (BBS) were the first "virtual" communities. These groups were based on the Unix operating system and referred to under the general term Usenet. The groups were arranged into major categories, such as "comp" for computer and "alt" for alternate.

The World Wide Web Is Spun

In 1980, Tim Berners-Lee, an independent contractor at the European Organization for Nuclear Research (CERN), Switzerland, built ENQUIRE, a personal database of people and software models, and began playing around with "hypertext"—each new page of information in ENQUIRE was linked to an existing page.

In 1984, Berners-Lee returned to CERN and considered one of its primary problems: Physicists from around the world needed to share data, but there were no commonalities with regard to machines and software. He wrote a proposal in March 1989 for a "web of nodes," "a large hypertext database with typed links," that could be viewed by "browsers" on a network, but it generated little interest. Mike Sendall, Berners-Lee's boss, encouraged him to begin implementing his system on a newly acquired NeXT workstation. His system was eventually dubbed the World Wide Web and was released in 1992.

Browsing Goes Mainstream

Mosaic, the first mainstream commercial browser, was developed by Marc Andreesen and Eric Bina. It combined the functions of Apple's HyperCard with hypertext capabilities. HyperCard was a precursor of the World Wide Web. It combined database capabilities with a graphical user interface. Mosaic was eventually revised to work with Windows and Mac computers and emerged as Netscape.

While the Internet and the Web were evolving, so were desktop computers. Computers were being used for word processing, databases, and spreadsheets. Laptop computers were introduced. Most historians consider the first true laptop computer to be the Osborne 1. Produced in 1981, it weighed 24 pounds and cost $1,795. The Osborne 1 came with a five-inch screen, modem port, two 5 1/4-inch floppy drives, a large collection of bundled software programs, and a battery pack.

The computer industry was growing and people were seeing the potential—the huge potential. As discussed above, companies like Dell, Compaq, and, of course, Microsoft emerged during this period.

Ruby and Java and Perl, Oh My!: Programming and Languages

Computers communicate in a binary-based language, also known as a machine language. With such languages (known today as first-generation languages), the programmer must input every command and all data in binary form. Such programming is tedious and time-consuming, to say the least. For example, a basic operation, such as comparing the contents of a register (a software component used to store information) to the data in a memory chip location might look like this: 11001010 00010111 11110101 00101011.

Assembly languages, also known as second-generation languages, were devised to simplify this process. By assigning a short, usually three-letter, mnemonic code to each machine-language command, assembly-language programs could be written and "debugged"—cleaned of logic and data errors—in a fraction of the time needed by machine-language programmers.

Assembly languages, however, can be used only with one type of CPU chip or microprocessor. This imposed a different set of limitations on programmers—they had to learn a new programming style each time they worked on a machine with different hardware. High-level, or third-generation, languages were invented to get around this problem. High-level languages often use words that are more like the English language—for example, LIST, PRINT, OPEN, and so on—as commands that represent a sequence of tens, or even hundreds, of machine-language instructions. The commands are entered from the keyboard or from a program in memory or in a storage device, and they are intercepted by a program that translates them into machine-language instructions.

Software writers (or programmers) use different languages, depending on the problem they are working to solve. These languages are essentially sequences of commands in the form of algorithms (an explicit set of instructions). Perhaps best known is the imperative, or procedural, language, which applies sequences of commands to manipulate data—the program is told what to do and

INTERVIEW

The Past Shaping the Future

Bill Weiss
Worldwide technical community director for Microsoft Services

How long have you been in this field? What drew you to it?
I have been in this field for 34 years, having been drawn to it initially by something I saw on a matchbook cover that said you could earn up to $350 per week operating a computer. I decided to go to my local technical college to get a computer science degree and launched my career from there.

How has the computer industry's past shaped its present? How do you think it will shape its future?
History shows us what has worked well and what does not work well. Shaping the future is, in part, taking what has worked well and refining it, or taking a completely new [tack] at solving that same problem. Oftentimes, we know what problems we want to solve with technology, but have to wait for technology to catch up. [For example,] things like speech recognition require computing power that was not there when the concept originated, but after technology advanced and computer power increased, it allowed for advancements in speech recognition.

how to do it. Declarative languages, on the other hand, simply tell the program what to do. This requires the programmer to define the problem more precisely so that the correct algorithm can be used.

Imperative and declarative languages comprise subsets of languages. Object-oriented programming, for example, is a type of imperative programming that uses "objects"—data structures that incorporate instructions, or "methods"—to design applications and computers programs. Rather than writing instructions for a task line by line, a programmer simply calls on an object to perform a task.

Types of declarative languages include functional and logical programming. Functional programming evaluates mathematical functions to solve problems. It emphasizes the evaluation of expressions (instructions), rather than execution of commands. These expressions are formed by using functions to combine basic values.

Logical programming uses backward reasoning to solve a problem, based on implications. Take, for example, a logical program that is designed to determine whether an alarm should sound if a temperature reading goes below a certain number. The implication is as follows: "If the alarm is sounded, the operator will know the temperature is below 45°F." The program turns this into the following procedure: "To tell the operator that the temperature is below 45°F, sound the alarm."

There is still another level to computer languages. Consider the following three groups (although there is some overlap among them):

Scripting languages: Most computer languages fall into this category. With a scripting language, information is usually interpreted instead of compiled. Scripting languages are often used to add functionality to Web pages. Examples include JavaScript, Perl, and Python.

"Internet languages": These languages are used to embed code inside an HTML page in order to combine statements and data. Examples include PHP and JavaScript.

Markup languages: These are designed for the processing, definition, and presentation of text. Markup languages use tags to define how text and other elements should appear on a Web page. Examples include HTML and XML.

In addition, there are many hybrid languages that encompass various aspects of the languages discussed previously. If you are interested in a specific language, you should explore it further on your own—dedicated Web sites, books, and even classes are all great starting points (see chapter 6).

Denis L. Sureau, the author of "History of Computer Languages and Their Evolution," has put together an extensive history of computer language. It is paraphrased briefly here. Where possible, the date the first working implementation was known about is provided. For more information, the article in its entirety can be found at http://www.scriptol.com/programming/history.php.

Autocode (1952) This is a symbolic, assembly-language code, implemented first on the Mark I computer.

Information Processing Language (1956) IPL is a low-level list-processing language that implements recursivity. Recursivity is one of the central tenets of computer science. It is a looping solution to a problem wherein the ultimate solution depends on solutions to smaller instances of the same problem.

FORmula TRANslator system (1954–1958) Known as FORTRAN, this language is dedicated to mathematical calculations. The 1958 iteration introduced functions or subroutines (portions of a program), loops, and a primitive FOR control structure (a control structure determines the order in which functions are carried out).

LISt Processing (1958–1960) Known as Lisp, this is a functional language for list processing. It is purely recursive and not iterative (it does not repeat a process in a computer program).

ALGOrithmic Language (1960–1968) Algol was the first universal language to be machine-independent. It introduced the concept of using blocks of statements and local variables inside a block, as well as dynamic arrays. (An array is a data structure consisting of a group of elements that are accessed by indexing.)

COmmon Business Oriented Language (1960) Cobol is a procedural language aimed at enterprise management, in which a program is divided into four divisions—identification, environment, data, procedure—which, in turn, can be divided into sections.

Beginner's All-purpose Symbolic Instruction Code (1964) BASIC is an easy-to-learn language. Apple, IBM, and Microsoft have all adapted it to their uses. Today, it has been largely replaced by C.

If You See What I Mean (1965) ISWIM was the first language to use lazy evaluation. Lazy evaluation is a technique whereby a computation in a program is not run until (and if) it is needed.

StroNg Oriented symBOlic Language (1967) SNOBOL was the first language to implement associative arrays indexed by any type of keys. It allows you to run code stored inside strings. Data types include string, integer, real, array, table, pattern, and user-defined.

Pascal (1970) Named after Blaise Pascal, this language was designed to ease the building of compilers and to encourage good programming practices by forcing the use of structured programming and data structuring. (A compiler takes code written in one computer language and transforms it into another.)

SmallTalk (1972) This is a fully object-oriented language that runs inside a graphical user interface environment, with windows and a mouse.

C (1973) C (and its variants) is one of the most popular programming languages due to its portability and speed. It allows for incremental compiling. It was also used to write Unix.

Prolog (1970) This declarative computer language introduced logic programming.

Standard Query Language (1970) SQL is the de facto language for relational databases. Relational databases group data according to common attributes.

C++ (1981–1986) This language is an object-oriented version of C that introduced the concept of operator overloading (assigning multiple meanings to the same operator, depending on context).

Practical Extracting and Report Language (1987) Perl, which includes lists and associative arrays, eventually replaced the command-line languages Unix, Sh, Sed, and Awk. It is used primarily for system administration and CGI scripts.

Python (1991) This scripting language with dynamic types was designed to replace Perl. It is object-oriented and can be extended with C libraries.

Ruby (1994) Ruby was designed to be clearer than Perl and to be more object-oriented than Python (although it retains many of Python's features). It is easily extensible. What sets this language apart is its ability to add methods (pieces of code associated with a class or object to perform a task) to instances (also called an object).

Java (1994) Java is a procedural language, similar to C++ (although simpler). It compiles in bytecode and can be interpreted on any computer. Unlike C and C++, Java has only dynamic arrays.

Personal Home Pages Hypertext Processor (1995) PHP is a multiplatform scripting language embedded inside HTML. It is similar to C; however, variables are prefixed by the $ symbol, as with Unix or Perl. With an extended library of functions, developers can use it to build dynamic Web pages.

JavaScript (1995) This is a scripting language designed to embed procedural code into Web pages. It can be used with other applications, such as XML-based language. Its syntax is similar to C and Java.

Unified Modeling Language (1996) UML combines three modeling languages and uses a graphical notation to design software projects. A source is a diagram expressing objects and their interactions. A model is made of views, and the combination of them describes a complete system. The model is abstract and domain-independent.

C# (2000) Pronounced "C-sharp," this is the main language of the .NET environment. It is simple to learn, object-oriented, and can be used to serve a variety of general purposes. C# uses a multilanguage library: the CLR (Common Language Runtime).

Aspect for Java (2001) AspectJ is a Java extension that implements aspect-oriented programming. The unit is not the class, but a concern that spans multiple classes (a concern is a particular set of behaviors needed by a computer program).

Scriptwriter-Oriented Language (2001) Scriptol is a language that can be used for applications, for scripting, and to make dynamic Web pages. Variables and literals are objects, and it uses XML as its internal data structure.

Scala (2004) This is an object-oriented language that implements some Python features in Java syntax. It is statically typed and both procedural and functional. It currently runs on JVM and .NET.

A Brief Chronology

The following is an annotated timeline of important dates and landmark events in the history of computing. A more extensive chronology, starting with 4000 B.C., can be found on the Institute of Electrical and Electronics Engineers (IEEE) Web site (see chapter 6).

1901: The appearance of the keypunch.

1915: The glimmerings of the microchip; physicist Manson Benedicks discovers that the germanium crystal can be used to convert alternating current (AC) to direct current (DC).

1924: CTR (Calculating, Tabulating & Recording Co.) is renamed IBM (International Business Machines).

1935: ISM introduces the 601 multiplying punch card machine.

1937: Howard Aiken submits a proposal to IBM for a digital calculating machine that can perform the four fundamental operations of arithmetic in an ordered sequence.

George Stibitz develops a binary circuit based on Boolean algebra.

1938: Hewlett-Packard is formed.

1941: The first fully functional, program-controlled electromechanical digital computer is introduced.

1943: Colossus, considered the first all-electronic calculating device, is introduced in Britain.

1945: ENIAC is fully functional.

1947: The magnetic drum memory is introduced as a data storage device for computers.

1949: The Whirlwind, considered the first real-time computer, is placed into service at MIT.

1949: John Mauchly develops Short Order Code, considered the first high-level programming language.

1952: The public at large becomes aware of computers when Univac I predicts (correctly) that Eisenhower would win that year's presidential election.

1953: The IBM 650 is the first mass-produced computer.

1954: Texas Instruments introduces the silicon transistor, which helps lower manufacturing costs.

1956: The concept of artificial intelligence is first introduced at a meeting at Dartmouth College.

1958: Bell develops the modem data phone, which enables telephone lines to transmit binary data.

1959: COBOL is created; Lisp is developed.

1960: The first commercial computer, employing a monitor and keyboard, is introduced.

1963: ASCII 7-bit code is accepted for the exchange of information.

1964: BASIC is developed; Cray, the world's first supercomputer, is unveiled; the mouse is invented; the first computer-aided design system is developed.

1968: Intel is established.

1969: Bell Labs begins to develop Unix; the first four nodes of Arpanet become functional.

1970: The floppy disk is introduced.

1971: The Intel 4004 microprocessor is introduced; the term "Silicon Valley" is coined; the first network-based e-mail message is sent.

1972: The C language is developed; word processing systems are introduced.

1976: The Apple I, consisting mostly of a circuit board, is developed by Steve Jobs and Steve Wozniak.

1977: Apple Computer is incorporated; Microsoft is founded.

1978: Intel's first 16-bit processor is introduced.

1981: The first "personal," portable computer, the Osborne I, is the size of a small suitcase and weighs 24 pounds.

1982: *Time* magazine names the computer the "Man of the Year"; commercial e-mail service is available in 25 cities.

1983: The global Internet is established with the completion of TCP/IP.

1984: The Macintosh is introduced, as is the CD-ROM; the term "cyberspace" is coined by author William Gibson.

1985: Windows I is introduced.

1988: The first worm is introduced on the Internet.

1989: Tim Berners-Lee publishes the World Wide Web project.

1993: Intel introduces the Pentium chip.

1994: Netscape's first browser becomes available, and growing numbers of people start surfing the Web.

1996: The Internet comes of age. Multimedia machines and digital cameras are now within reach of the average consumer.

2000: The "Millennium Bug" or "Y2K Bug" causes minor disturbances, but not the worldwide disasters some pundits foretold.

2002: Quantum computing is beginning to be explored. Hewlett-Packard merges with Compaq Computer forming the second largest IT company on earth.

2004: The Google search engine indexes 3,307,998,701 Web pages. Spam takes up an estimated 33 percent of Internet traffic. More than 650 million PCs are in use worldwide.

2005: Google indexes more than 8 billion Web pages. The MIT Media Lab, in conjunction with the nonprofit association, One Laptop per Child (OLPC) launches a new research initiative to develop a $100 laptop, with the aim of revolutionizing how children worldwide are educated.

2006: There are now more than 100 million Web sites on the Internet.

2009: Social networking sites came of age with popularity of Facebook and Twitter coverage of Iranian election protests.

Computers may be designed to perform millions of calculations, but don't mistake them for giant calculators. Their capabilities and applications have gone far, far beyond that. Computers can simulate—sometimes in real time—complex phenomena, such as where an approaching hurricane will land and how extensive it will be, or how a deadly virus will spread through the population.

The need for which computers was originally designed—to perform calculations faster than a human—became more complex as the potential for this amazing machine was better understood. It's quite possible that Turing, Aiken, Pascal, and the rest could never have foreseen the many and far-reaching uses computers have today. In an attempt to foresee where computers are going next, it's important to understand the state of the industry as it exists right now. Chapter 2 provides a current overview of the computer industry—from its economic effect to the major players to the working environment, after reading this chapter, you will better understand the strength and viability of this industry.

State of the Industry

In its early years, the computer industry was focused more on computers themselves—making them faster, smaller, more efficient—rather than on using them to solve real-world problems. Furthermore, when first conceived, computers were thought to only have any real relevance for business, industry, and government entities—and perhaps universities. Today, the trend is to turn nearly any everyday device—cell phone, car, washing machine, hot water heater—into a computer. This is not to say that the focus has moved away from the actual computer. Rather, as the device's potential continues to expand and evolve, new ways of thinking about what a "computer" is and how it looks are also emerging.

The field of computer science is changing rapidly, as it always has. This chapter will provide an overview of this aspect of the computer industry by exploring various statistics related to employment and wages, current and future trends, key conferences and industry events, the difference between working for a large company versus a smaller one, and more. The most common areas in which people typically work in this field are discussed in depth here. To learn about other related positions, see Chapter 3: On the Job.

Trends in Employment and Wages

According to the U.S. Department of Labor, programmers and software developers are employed in almost every industry, but the largest concentration is in computer systems design and related services.

Large numbers also work for software publishers, financial institutions, insurance carriers, educational institutions, government agencies, and other companies and enterprises. Many computer programmers work independently as consultants on a temporary or contract basis, some of whom are self-employed (about 17,000 computer programmers were self-employed in 2006). Computer programmers held about 435,000 jobs in 2006. An estimated 8 out of 10 held an associate's degree or higher in 2006; nearly half held a bachelor's degree, and 2 out of 10 held a graduate degree.

Jobs for programmers should be most plentiful in computer consulting businesses. These businesses are part of the computer systems design and related services industry, which is projected to be among the fastest-growing industries in the economy over the 2006 to 2016 period.

Prospects for advancement as a computer programmer are good—provided one keeps up-to-date with the latest technology. This is not a field for someone who does not thrive on change and who has a hard time learning to adapt. Some applications programmers may move into systems programming after they gain experience and take courses in systems software. With general business experience, programmers may become programmer-analysts or systems analysts, or may be promoted to managerial positions. Programmers with specialized knowledge and experience with a language or operating system may work in research and development, and may even become computer software engineers.

The employment of computer programmers is expected to decline by 4 percent through 2016. However, because computer programmers can transmit their programs over the Internet, they can perform their job from anywhere in the world, allowing companies to employ workers in countries that have lower prevailing wages.

Computer programmers are at a much higher risk of having their jobs outsourced than are workers involved in more complex and sophisticated functions, such as software engineering. Much of the work of computer programmers requires little localized or specialized knowledge and can be made routine once a particular programming language is mastered.

Nevertheless, local programmers will always be needed. Employers especially value programmers who understand how their role fits into the company's overall business and objectives. Demand will likely grow for programmers with strong object-oriented programming capabilities and technical specialization in areas such as client/

server programming (writing programs that communicate with other computer programs across a network), wireless applications, multimedia technology, and graphic user interface.

Despite the projected decline, numerous job openings will result from the need to replace programmers who leave the labor force or who transfer to other occupations. Prospects likely will be best for applicants with a bachelor's degree and experience with a variety of programming languages and tools. The languages that are in demand today include C++, Java, and other object-oriented languages, as well as newer, domain-specific languages that apply to computer networking, database management, and Internet application development. As always, the computer programmer who stays up-to-date on the technology is the programmer with the edge.

Median annual earnings of computer programmers were $65,510 in May 2006. The middle 50 percent earned between $49,580 and $85,080 a year. The lowest 10 percent earned less than $38,460, and the highest 10 percent earned more than $106,610. Median annual earnings in the industries employing the largest numbers of computer programmers in May 2006 are as follows:

Software publishers: $79,270
Computer systems design and related services: $67,880
Management of companies and enterprises: $67,170
Insurance carriers: $65,650

According to the National Association of Colleges and Employers, starting salary offers for computer programmers averaged $49,928 per year in 2007, and according to Robert Half Technology, a firm providing specialized staffing services, average annual starting salaries in 2007 ranged from $55,250 to $90,250 for applications development programmers/analysts, and from $60,250 to $94,750 for software developers. Average starting salaries for mainframe systems programmers ranged from $52,250 to $70,750.

Computer systems analysts held about 504,000 jobs in 2006. Although they are increasingly employed in every sector of the economy, the greatest concentration of these workers is in the design of computer systems and related industries. A growing number are employed on a temporary or contract basis; many of these individuals are self-employed, working independently as contractors or consultants. About 29,000 computer systems analysts were self-employed in 2006.

Best
Practice

Always expect the unexpected. This is true in any area of life, but is of special importance for computer programmers. It's important to consider all possible situations under which a program will run and anticipate any errors that could result. While these contingencies can vary widely, based on the computer language being used and the purpose for which the code is being written, an example that is common to Java programmers has to do with null pointer. A pointer is a data type whose value points to another value elsewhere in the program; therefore, a null error is aimed at an empty location. While sometimes null pointers are used deliberately, in many cases, they are not. Furthermore, this is not something that will ordinarily be detected until the program is run, so check and double-check those return values, and you may save yourself a world of trouble later on.

This field is expected to grow by 29 percent from 2006 to 2016. In addition, the 146,000 new jobs that are expected to arise will be substantial. Demand for systems analysts will increase as organizations adopt and integrate increasingly sophisticated technologies. One possible trend has to do with wireless capabilities and the growth of personal mobile computers—whether it's a laptop, a PDA, or a phone. These technologies have created a need for new systems that can integrate them into existing networks. Explosive growth in these areas is expected to fuel demand for analysts who are knowledgeable about systems integration and network, data, and communications security.

As with other information technology jobs, employment growth may be tempered somewhat as some analyst jobs are outsourced. Firms may look to cut costs by shifting operations to foreign countries with lower prevailing wages and highly educated workers who have strong technical skills. However, this is not expected to be as prevalent as with more general careers, such as computer programmers.

Job prospects in this field are expected to be good. As with computer programmers and other computer-specific positions, job openings will occur as a result of strong growth and from the need to replace workers who move into managerial positions or other occupations, or who leave the labor force. As technology becomes more sophisticated and complex, employers demand a higher level of skill and expertise from their employees. People with the best prospects are those with an advanced degree in computer science or computer engineering, or with an MBA with a concentration in information systems. College graduates with a bachelor's degree in computer science, computer engineering, information science, or management information systems also should enjoy favorable job prospects, particularly if they have practical experience to back up their academic learning.

Median annual earnings of computer systems analysts were $69,760 in May 2006. The middle 50 percent earned between $54,320 and $87,600 a year. The lowest 10 percent earned less than $42,780, and the highest 10 percent earned more than $106,820. Median annual earnings in the industries employing the largest numbers of computer systems analysts in May 2006 were as follows:

Professional and commercial equipment
and supplies merchant wholesalers: $81,080
Computer systems design and related services: $71,680
Management of companies and enterprises: $71,090
Insurance carriers: $69,990
State governments: $61,340

According to the National Association of Colleges and Employers, starting offers for graduates with a bachelor's degree in computer science averaged $53,396. Starting offers for graduates with a bachelor's degree in information sciences and systems averaged $50,852. For those with a degree in management information systems/business data processing, starting offers averaged $47,648.

According to Robert Half Technology, starting salaries for systems analysts ranged from $64,000 to $87,000 in 2007. Starting salaries for business systems analysts ranged from $61,250 to $86,500. Starting salaries for developer/programmer analysts ranged from $55,250 to $90,250.

Computer software engineers held about 857,000 jobs in 2006. Approximately 507,000 were computer applications software engineers, and about 350,000 were computer systems software engineers. Although they are employed in most industries, the largest concentration of computer software engineers—more than 29 percent—is in computer systems design and related services. About 17,000 computer software engineers were self-employed in 2006.

Employment of computer software engineers is projected to increase by 38 percent over the 2006 to 2016 period, which is much faster than the average for all occupations. This occupation is expected to generate about 324,000 new jobs—one of the largest employment increases of any occupation.

In May 2006, median annual earnings of computer applications software engineers were $79,780. The middle 50 percent earned between $62,830 and $98,470. The lowest 10 percent earned less than $49,350, and the highest 10 percent earned more than $119,770. Median annual earnings in the industries employing the largest numbers of computer applications software engineers in May 2006 were as follows:

Software publishers: $84,560
Computer systems design and related services: $78,850
Management, scientific, and technical
consulting services: $78,850
Management of companies and enterprises: $78,580
Insurance carriers: $74,230

In May 2006, median annual earnings of computer systems software engineers were $85,370. The middle 50 percent earned between $67,620 and $105,330. The lowest 10 percent earned less than $53,580, and the highest 10 percent earned more than $125,750. Median annual earnings in the industries employing the largest numbers of computer systems software engineers in May 2006 are as follows:

Research and development in the physical,
engineering, and life sciences: $97,220
Scientific research and development services: $97,180
Computer and peripheral equipment manufacturing: $93,240
Software publishers: $87,450
Computer systems design and related services: $84,660
Data processing, hosting, and related services: $78,270

According to the National Association of Colleges and Employers, starting salary offers for graduates with a bachelor's degree in computer engineering averaged $56,201 in 2007. Starting salary offers for graduates with a bachelor's degree in computer science averaged $53,396.

According to Robert Half Technology, starting salaries for software engineers in software development ranged from $66,500 to

$99,750 in 2007. For network engineers, starting salaries ranged from $65,750 to $90,250.

Database administrators held about 119,000 jobs in May 2006. The greatest concentration of these workers is in the computer systems design and related services industry. A growing number are employed on a temporary or contract basis; many of these individuals are self-employed, working independently as contractors or consultants.

This occupation is expected to grow 37 percent from 2006 to 2016, as organizations continue to adopt and integrate increasingly sophisticated technologies. Job increases will be driven by rapid growth in computer systems design and related services, which is projected to be one of the fastest growing industries in the U.S. economy.

Those with an advanced degree in computer science or computer engineering, or with an MBA with a concentration in information systems should enjoy favorable employment prospects. Applicants with a bachelor's degree in computer science, computer engineering, information science, or management information systems (MIS) also should enjoy favorable prospects, particularly if they have supplemented their formal education with practical experience.

Median annual earnings of database administrators were $64,670 in May 2006. The middle 50 percent earned between $48,560 and $84,830. The lowest 10 percent earned less than $37,350, and the highest 10 percent earned more than $103,010. In May 2006, median annual earnings of database administrators employed in computer systems design and related services were $72,510, and for those in management of companies and enterprises, earnings were $67,680.

Median annual earnings of network/systems administrators were $64,600 in May 2006. The middle 50 percent earned between $49,510 and $82,630. The lowest 10 percent earned less than $38,410, and the highest 10 percent earned more than $101,740. Median annual earnings in the industries employing the largest numbers of network systems and data communications analysts in May 2006 are as follows:

Wired telecommunications carriers: $72,480
Management of companies and enterprises: $68,490
Management, scientific, and technical
consulting services: $67,830
Computer systems design and related services: $67,080
State governments: $52,020

Everyone
Knows

There are five generations of computer languages. First-generation computers relied on machine language, the lowest-level programming language understood by computers, to perform operations, and could only solve one problem at a time. Input was based on punched cards and paper tape; output was displayed on printouts. Examples include the UNIVAC and ENIAC computers.

Second-generation computers still relied on punched cards for input and printouts for output, but moved from a binary machine language to symbolic, or assembly, languages, which allowed programmers to specify instructions in words. High-level programming languages were also being developed at this time, such as early versions of COBOL and FORTRAN. These were also the first computers to store their instructions in their memory, which moved from a magnetic drum to magnetic core technology.

Instead of punched cards and printouts, users interacted with third-generation computers through keyboards and monitors and with an operating system, which allowed the device to run many different applications at one time with a central program that monitored the memory.

The microprocessor heralded the fourth generation of computers, with thousands of integrated circuits being built onto a single silicon chip. A prime example is the Intel 4004 chip: It contained all of the components of the computer—from the central processing unit and memory to input/output controls—within it. This generation also saw the development of graphical user interfaces, the mouse, and handheld devices.

Fifth-generation computing devices, based on artificial intelligence, are still in development, though some applications, such as voice recognition, are in use today. Additional fields of study include quantum computers and molecular and nanotechnology. The goal of fifth-generation computing is to develop devices that respond to natural language input and are capable of learning and self-organization.

The U.S. Bureau of Labor Statistics does not report any separate employment figures for Web site designers. Rather, they combine employment statistics for computer systems analysts, database administrators, and computer scientists, which includes Web site designers. According to Education Online Search, based on the large number of people reported in this group as a whole—almost 1 million people—it is safe to assume that there are more than 100,000 Web site designers in the United States.

According to the Bureau of Labor Statistics, Web site design can be expected to be among the fastest growing occupations through 2012, with employment expected to grow much faster than the average. As might be expected, outsourcing is slowing down job growth and creating greater competition for available jobs; however, this should not discourage the passionate, motivated Web site designer.

The Bureau of Labor Statistics did report that in 2003, the income range for Web site designers was between $51,250 and $73,750. An InfoWorld 2004 compensation survey placed Web site designer incomes at around $61,000. According to the Virginia Career Education Foundation, the average income is around $59,000.

Computer support specialists held about 552,000 jobs in 2006. Although they worked in a wide range of industries, about 23 percent were employed in professional, scientific, and technical services industries, principally computer systems design and related services. Substantial numbers of these workers were also employed in:

Administrative and support services companies
Financial institutions
Insurance companies
Government agencies
Educational institutions
Software publishers
Telecommunications organizations
Healthcare organizations
Management of companies and enterprises

Employment of computer support specialists is expected to increase by 13 percent from 2006 to 2016, which is about as fast as the average for all occupations. Demand for these workers will result as organizations and individuals continue to adopt increasingly sophisticated technology. Job growth will continue to be driven by the ongoing expansion of the computer system design and related services industry, which is projected to remain one of the fastest-growing industries in the U.S. economy. As computers and software become more complex, support specialists will be needed to provide technical assistance to customers and other users. As with other positions in this field, the adoption of new mobile technologies will continue to create a need for these workers to familiarize and educate computer users. Consulting jobs for computer support specialists also should continue to increase as businesses seek help managing, upgrading, and customizing computer systems that are becoming ever more complex.

Median annual earnings of computer support specialists were $41,470 in May 2006. The middle 50 percent earned between $32,110 and $53,640. The lowest 10 percent earned less than $25,290, and the highest 10 percent earned more than $68,540. Median annual earnings in the industries employing the largest numbers of computer support specialists in May 2006 were as follows:

Software publishers: $46,270
Management of companies and enterprises: $42,770
Computer systems design and related services: $42,510
Colleges, universities, and professional schools: $40,130
Elementary and secondary schools: $37,880

According to Robert Half Technology, starting salaries in 2007 ranged from $27,500 to $37,000 for help-desk workers.

Where Does the Future Lie?

The interesting thing about the computer industry is that the future is not always where it is anticipated to be. Certainly, trends can be anticipated and partially predicted, but the future really isn't known until it arrives. For example, in 1976, when technicians were working on disk drives the size of washing machines that held 20 megabytes of storage, who could have imagined a device the size of a deck of playing cards that held the equivalent of 6,000 of those washing-machine–sized devices just a mere 20 to 30 years later?

So while the future of computing may not be something anyone can know for certain, there are areas that show promise and that offer interesting possibilities. The person reading this book who is brand new to this field may be the person who takes an area like artificial intelligence or quantum computing a direction no one else could have anticipated. Perhaps in another 25 to 30 years, that card-sized device will be the size of a postage stamp and have 10,000 times the capabilities.

New growth areas will also continue to arise from rapidly evolving technologies. The increasing uses of the Internet, the proliferation of Web sites, and mobile technology such as wireless Internet have created a demand for a wide variety of new products. Networking is a growing trend in this industry, and the ability to share information, the expansion of client-server environments, and the need for computer specialists to use their knowledge and skills in a problem-solving capacity will be major factors in the rising demand for database administrators, as is the case for computer programmers.

Artificial Intelligence

Artificial intelligence (AI) may well be the Holy Grail of computing. The term was first coined in 1956 by an American computer scientist named John McCarthy. He defined it as "the science and engineering of making intelligent machines." In essence, AI refers to creating computers that have the ability to learn, understand, recognize, and reason, much as humans do. The research is extensive; however, it has produced little in the way of solid results—yet. One exception is expert systems. A type of knowledge-based system, this is a computer system that has been programmed with the knowledge and intuition of human experts in a given field. These systems advise technicians, researchers, and others on such diverse tasks as troubleshooting communications networks, analyzing spectrograms, and diagnosing illness.

But can a computer—a machine—truly be created to act like a human being? The primary difficulty with this concept lies in the complex, multifaceted nature of the human mind and the multilayered levels of understanding inherent within it. According to Alan Turing, a British computer scientist, mathematician, logician and cryptanalyst, the intelligence of any machine can only be assessed by observing its behavior. If a person thinks the machine is intelligent, it is. This concept is demonstrated in what is known as the Turing Test. In this test, a human evaluator engages in two natural-language conversations: one with another human and one with a machine. If, based on the responses, the human evaluator cannot tell the difference between the human and the machine, the machine is said to have passed the test and to have demonstrated intelligence. (There are criticisms and problems with this test, to be sure. Readers are encouraged to turn to chapter 6 for books that address the topic of artificial intelligence more thoroughly.)

The bottom line is that for all that computers can appear to behave as humans, at this point in time, the human brain is still superior and can do things a computer just can't do. AI research has made some progress at imitating this kind of reasoning and problem solving, but when a human hears the word "dog," for example, he or she may think of a medium-sized animal with two ears, four legs, a tail, and that barks. But that picture isn't true for all dogs. For all these advances in this field, computers still operate on logic. A human has common sense; a computer does not. A human knows that there are all sorts of exceptions in the world; a computer does not. And then there's the paradox: If a human being creates a computer that can behave exactly like the human brain, is the computer now smarter than the human? Can a human create something artificial that is exactly like it without surpassing it?

Cloud Computing

American computer scientist John McCarthy also had a hand promoting this concept. McCarthy believed that "computation may someday be organized as a public utility." This involves using the Internet to meet the needs of users; it's a network, of sorts, that goes beyond what a traditional network is and can do. Cloud computing is designed to meet an ever-present need: more resources and an easy way to increase capacity without increasing cost. This field is still in the early stages of development, and the industry is still debating what it is, exactly, and how it can best be achieved. In one form, called "software as a service" (SaaS), it involves the distribution of a single application to thousands of users—an example is Google Apps, a single product with several services, such as e-mail, word processing, and chat, built into it. Another form, called utility computing, involves the use of virtual servers and storage areas. IT departments, for example, find these convenient—extra storage that doesn't take up physical space. One of the most appealing traits of cloud computing is that users do not need to have any special knowledge or skills to use the technology—it's just there, so to speak—in "the clouds."

Green IT

Practically everyone these days is aware of how important it is to recycle, to minimize the carbon footprint, to consume less, to be "green"—and computing is no different. Green IT, also called green computing, is focused on using computer resources more efficiently. The goals of green IT are to reduce the use of hazardous materials in the production of computer parts, maximize energy efficiency during a product's lifetime, and promote the creation of recyclable products and components, where possible, or even products that are biodegradable. At the same time, user satisfaction and computing ability and performance must not be sacrificed—a fine line to walk, indeed!

One of the earliest pushes in this direction was the U.S. Environmental Protection Agency's EnergyStar program. This voluntary labeling program was designed to promote and recognize energy efficiency in monitors, among other things, and results in the introduction and adoption of "sleep mode," whereby when a computer was not in use for a designated period, it would minimize the amount of energy it used without shutting itself completely off.

Cloud computing and green IT are linked, in a way. By making more resources virtual and minimizing the amount of energy needed to produce, package, ship, store, house, and maintain physical computers, their components, and related equipment, more can be done with less. People who are new to the computer industry and who also have a passion for the environment may find working in green IT especially appealing. Creating smaller components that are faster and more efficient, devising new materials that aren't as hazardous (that perhaps are completely nontoxic), and recycling and reusing components wherever possible—even telecommuting—helps ensure that our world is a clean, enjoyable place for years and years to come.

Quantum Computing

Quantum mechanics is a branch of physics that describes physical systems at the microscopic level—it deals with atomic and subatomic systems. In fact, it was designed to provide a better explanation of the atom. The field of quantum computing is still very much in its infancy, but by harnessing these principles into a computer, the hope is that quantum computers will be able to perform calculations millions of times faster than traditional computers. Unlike silicon-based computers, quantum computers would use the power of atoms and molecules to perform calculations and carry out tasks. Traditional computers operate in two states—the binary system—information is represented as either a 1 or a 0. Quantum computers, on the other hand are not limited to two states; they encode information as quantum bits (qubits), which represent atoms, ions, photons, or electrons. Because a quantum computer can contain multiple states simultaneously, it has the potential to be millions of times more powerful than today's most powerful supercomputers.

An in-depth look at quantum computing is well beyond the scope of this book. However, chapter 6 provides readers with sources of more information.

Web 2.0

The World Wide Web has gone far beyond anyone's wildest imaginings (well, perhaps Tim Berners-Lee, its creator, could have foreseen these developments). The Web has exploded beyond what, at its heart, was just a giant network of hyperlinked pages, to a truly global collaboration. Today, "Web 2.0" has emerged. Rather than referring to a new set of technologies, as one might initially think upon hearing the term, it refers to a so-called second generation of Web development and design that encompasses things like blogs, wikis, social networking sites, hosted services, and Web communities.

Andrew McAfee, associate professor of business administration at Harvard University, uses the acronym SLATES to refer to Web 2.0 Web sites. Their features include:

Search: The ease of finding information through keyword search, which makes the platform valuable.

Links: Guides to important pieces of information. The best pages are those most frequently linked to.

Authoring: The ability to create constantly updating content over a platform that is shifted from being the creation of a few to being the constantly updated, interlinked work. Take wikis, for example. The content is constantly changing because people are constantly undoing and redoing each other's work.

Tags: The categorization of content by creating tags that are simple, one-word descriptions to facilitate searching and avoid rigid, premade categories.

Extensions: The automation of some of the work and pattern matching by using algorithms (this is the basis of data mining).

Signals: The use of RSS (Really Simple Syndication) technology to notify users with any changes of the content by sending e-mails to them. (RSS is a format in which works that are updated often, like a blog, are published.)

Some criticize the concept of Web 2.0, claiming that it is not really a "new" Web at all—merely new uses for old technologies. In fact, Tim Berners-Lee described Web 2.0 as "a piece of jargon," saying, "Nobody really knows what it means... [I]f Web 2.0 for you is blogs and wikis, then that is people to people. But that was what the Web was supposed to be all along." Whether one agrees with him or not, the fact remains that the Web has changed how we communicate, how we conduct business, how we live our lives—and more changes, perhaps still as yet unforeseen changes—certainly lie ahead.

So What Does It All Mean?

The business world moves in cycles, just like everything else, and the computer industry is certainly no exception. According to data gathered by Global Insight, Inc. and published by the World Information Technology and Services Alliance (WITSA), the worldwide market for information and communications technologies and services was estimated at more than $3 trillion in 2006, growing to $3.7 trillion in 2008. That number is expected to grow to more than $4 trillion by 2011. Annual growth in global information and communications technologies and services was estimated at 10.3 percent for both 2007 and 2008, but is expected to slow to 3.6 percent by 2011.

According to research firm IDC, sales through 2008 were relatively strong for items such as notebook computers and smaller "netbooks" (small, portable laptop computers primarily designed for sending e-mail and browsing the Web), along with advanced, Internet-enabled cell phones with color screens, electronic game players, MP3 players, digital cameras, servers, and other types of consumer and business electronics.

Plunkett Research, Ltd., a leading provider of industry-sector analysis and research, industry trends, and industry statistics, predicts that emerging markets will become more important to the IT sector. According to their research, the computing industry is entering what they call the "Broadband" or "Convergence Age." They use this term to describe the high-speed, constant access to information and media that even household users can enjoy, thanks to wi-fi, cable modems, and fiber-optic Internet connections. The result, as Plunkett Research sees it, is "a widespread convergence of entertainment, telephony, and computerized information: data, voice, and video, delivered to a rapidly evolving array of Internet appliances, PDAs, wireless devices (including cellular telephones), and desktop computers." According to their research, broadband access was installed in more than 120 million U.S. households in 2008, which led to increased demand for new Internet-delivered services, information, and entertainment. As a result, the ways in which software applications are accessed and used is changing. Consider Software as a Service (SaaS), for example. In the "old days," if one wanted a new operating system, software application or computer game, one had to go to a computer store and purchase it. In some cases, this software could be purchased online, but there was still time involved in shipping and waiting for the item to be delivered. With SaaS, the interested buyer can purchase the software online and download it directly to his or her computer.

Over the next five to ten years, Plunkett Research estimates the introduction of "significant groundbreaking products" in areas such as high-density storage, artificial intelligence, optical switches, and networking technologies, and quantum computing, to name a few. In addition, cheaper, faster chips and software that is more powerful will continue to enter the market at "blinding speed."

So what does this mean for the person entering the computer and programming industry today? Regardless of where someone enters this field—a large company or a small company, a programmer, network admin, or technical support technician—the odds are good that the way the job is being done now and the tools that are currently available will change dramatically in the next five to ten years. The best way to succeed is to find a passion, find a niche, learn all that can be learned about it, always be open to new ideas, and see where it all takes you.

Who Are the Major Players, and Where Are the Jobs?

Of course, there are the big companies—Microsoft, Google, Amazon, Adobe, IBM, Intel, RealNetworks, Apple, and Cisco—however, opportunities abound in this industry. Where there is a computer, there is a job.

When it comes to software, Microsoft and Apple are still the dominant names, but not the only ones. Linux, an open-source operating system created by Linus Torvalds at the University of Helsinki in Finland in 1991, has slowly and steadily earned a reputation as a reliable alternative for business computing. While Linux is available for free on the Internet, companies like Red Hat have made a business

On the Cutting Edge

Everyone has heard the phrase "with just a click of a mouse," but how about "with just a blink of the eye?" While eye tracking, a gaze-based means of interacting with Web sites, has been around for decades, it's a technology that has been prone with errors and was limited primarily to people whose physical disabilities kept them from using a keyboard and mouse. What's more, it wasn't precise enough to allow for a viewer's gaze to click a link, for example. Today, not only is the technology more accurate, but, according to Ted Selker, associate professor at the MIT Media and Arts Technology Laboratory and director of the Context Aware Computing Lab, "Things like eye tracking are using channels of communication that literally were unavailable to interface designers even five years ago." Selker says eye tracking might become standard on computers within the next five years. For now, the primary obstacle is the high cost of eye-tracking hardware.

out of packaging and providing support for Linux. IBM, Hewlett-Packard, and other notable companies have adopted Linux for use as a server platform, and the system is being used more and more as an operating system for home and desktop operating systems.

The term "productivity" is a catch-all term that refers to the work people do on computers. It encompasses everything from database entry and management to word processing, accounting, spreadsheet applications, presentations, graphic design, and more. Key players in the world of productivity include Microsoft, of course (nearly everyone is familiar with Microsoft Office), as well as Adobe (makers of Photoshop and Acrobat, among other things) and Autodesk (a manufacturer of 2-D and 3-D design software for use in architecture, engineering and building construction, manufacturing, and media and entertainment; AutoCAD is its most well-known product). OpenOffice.org, an open-source office suite that makes use of Linux, aims to compete with Microsoft Office and emulate its look and feel. The program, which is available for free on the Internet, can read and write most of the file formats found in Microsoft Office, as well as many other applications—most important, users have discovered it can open files of older versions of Microsoft Office programs and damaged files that newer versions of Microsoft Office programs cannot open.

When considering a career in this field, Ramon Infante suggests people look to where companies are focusing their research. Look at the annual reports for these companies and see where the research and development (R&D) money is going. That can alert you to future trends by showing you where companies are strategically placing their bets. Job fairs, schools and other training facilities, and conferences are also good sources of information. Find a niche that interests you, that you believe you can be passionate about, and pursue that passion.

Bill Weiss has additional advice: "If you look at the entire industry, you would get overwhelmed and intimidated. Pick a specific area that interests you...there are many different skills involved with something that, on the surface, seems to be a small slice of the computer industry, such as helping customers deploy a software program or application. There are complicated deployment tools, application compatibility testing, operating system image creation... find a niche where you can establish some credibility and let that credibility open more doors of opportunity."

Across the board, managers, developers, testers, and others who were interviewed for this book echoed the same general sentiment when it came to ideal strengths and talents a person needed to succeed in this field: initiative, determination, and a passion for technology. As the preceding sections explained, while there certainly are people in the computer world who have managed to create successful careers without a college education, having a bachelor's degree, at the very least, certainly gives the motivated career launcher an edge. A graduate's degree is strongly encouraged. In lieu of relevant degrees, experience is a factor employers consider, but that is a harder path to take. Self-taught computer mavens certainly exist, but they had to work that much harder than the people who combined experience with a college education.

When considering where to work, as mentioned, it helps to know a little about the companies under consideration. Some of the more notable names in the computer industry are examined here.

Adobe Systems

According to information on the Adobe Systems Web site, as of February 2009, Adobe has 7,173 employees, about 40 percent of whom work in San Jose (the company's headquarters). Adobe also has major development operations in Seattle, Washington; San Francisco, California; Ottawa, Ontario; Minneapolis, Minnesota; Newton, Massachusetts; San Luis Obispo, California; Hamburg, Germany; Noida, India; Bangalore, India; Bucharest, Romania; Beijing, China. In 2003, *Fortune* magazine rated Adobe as the fifth-best U.S. company to work for; however, by 2009, it had slipped to number 11.

Apple, Inc.

Of course, the company is best known for its Macintosh computer, iPod, and iPhone, but Apple also produces the Mac OS X operating system, the iTunes media browser, the iLife suite of multimedia and creativity software, the iWork suite of productivity software, and Final Cut Studio, a suite of professional audio and film-industry software products. The competition between these two companies has certainly extended to its consumers, with devoted fans singing the praises of Apple—and the pitfalls of Windows—to anyone who will listen. Whether you are a Mac or a PC, there is no denying the company is a presence in the industry, and likely to remain so. Headquartered in Cupertino, California, Apple has about 35,000 employees worldwide, according to an October 21, 2008 press release, and had worldwide annual sales of $32.48 billion in its fiscal year ending September 29, 2008. In 2008, *Fortune* magazine named Apple the most admired company in the United States after polling more than 3,700 people from dozens of industries on the companies they admire most.

Dell, Inc.

Headquartered in Round Rock, Texas, Dell currently employs more than 82,700 worldwide and earned $61.133 billion in revenue, according to its 2008 annual report. As of 2008, Dell was second in computer sales behind Hewlett Packard (HP). Dell currently sells personal computers, servers, data storage devices, network switches, software, and computer peripherals, as well as HDTVs (high-definition TVs) that are manufactured by other brands.

Dell now has the largest market share of any computer manufacturer, a position it carved out for itself starting in the year 2000. As competition increased among computer manufacturers, the company was founded on the notion that by selling PCs directly to the consumer, the consumer's needs could be better understood, thereby providing them with the most effective computing solution to meet those needs. It is a belief that has served the company well.

Between the second quarter of fiscal year 2001 and second quarter of fiscal year 2002, Dell's market share grew from 12.8 percent to 14.8 percent. At the same time, the combined market share of Hewlett-Packard and Compaq slipped from 17.9 percent to 15.1 percent. According to a 2006 press release, Dell is one of 38 high-performance companies in the S&P 500 that has consistently outperformed the market over the previous 15 years.

Google, Inc.

Headquartered in Mountain View, California (the name of Google's headquarters is the Googolplex), as of December 31, 2008, the company had 20,222 full-time employees, according to a press release issued in January 2009, and *Fortune* magazine has ranked it as the number one best place to work multiple times, the most recent being in 2007. Arguably one of the most recognizable brand names today, Google earns its money from advertising related to its Internet search, e-mail, online mapping, office productivity, social networking, and video sharing services, as well as selling advertising-free versions of the same technologies. When Google emerged as an Internet search engine, the concept behind it was revolutionary and changed the landscape of search forever—namely, that the pages with the most links to them from other highly relevant Web pages must be the most relevant pages associated with the search. According to recent annual reports, 99 percent of Google's revenue is derived from its advertising programs. For the 2006 fiscal year, the company reported $10.492 billion in total advertising revenues and $112 million in licensing and other revenues. An estimated 20,222 people work at Google, according to their December 21, 2008 annual report. While the company has been criticized for its below-average pay, the competitive compensation packages offered are viewed by some to offset this.

IBM

With a history dating back to the 19th century, International Business Machines (IBM) has earned its reputation as the world's largest computer company and the second largest software company. According to the company's Web site, IBM has more than 388,000 employees in more than 170 countries, eight research laboratories worldwide, and holds more patents than any other U.S.-based technology company. IBM employees have earned three Nobel Prizes, four Turing Awards, five National Medals of Technology, and five National Medals of Science.

INTERVIEW

So What Is the Future?

Ramon (Ray) Infante
Worldwide community director for unified communications, Microsoft

How has the computer industry's past shaped its present? How do you think it will shape its future?
Look how the future workforce is communicating. That will tell you what they will expect and require when they become workforce members themselves. They will show you where technology is going.

As individuals and businesses rely more on handheld computers and wireless networks, it will be necessary to integrate current computer systems with this new, more mobile technology. Mobility—in particular, how to extend the reach of a given platform into mobile space, for example, or extended cell phone capabilities from a system perspective—is a trend someone starting out in this industry should consider. Social networking is another area. Consider text messaging, for example. Given that it is quicker than e-mail and is often used by today's twenty-something users in lieu of e-mail or even an actual phone call, technology and social networking can be linked or leveraged in ways that have yet to be determined. The question someone entering this field needs to ask himself or herself is: Looking at technology today and how it is used, what are the applications for it in

Microsoft Corporation
Microsoft, headquartered in Redmond, Washington, has been the target of criticism for its monopoly-like business practices, but no one can doubt the company's clout. According to the company's annual report for 2005, Microsoft's reach extends to the MSNBC cable television network and the MSN Internet portal, and the company markets both computer hardware products, such as the Microsoft mouse, and home entertainment products, such as the Xbox, Xbox 360, Zune, and MSN TV. According to the Microsoft Web site, as of December 31, 2008, the company employed 95,828 people worldwide, 57,588 of whom were in the United States. In 2005, Microsoft received a 100 percent rating in the Corporate Equality Index from the Human Rights Campaign, a ranking of companies by how progressive the organization deems their policies concerning lesbian, gay, bisexual, and transsexual employees.

the future? Sometimes, that requires thinking outside the box—way outside the box.

What changes have you seen in this field since your first job? Could you have predicted them?
Outsourcing has changed the computing field. Today, most development and programming work is outsourced to developing markets—India, for example. However, jobs in software engineering and database administration are less prone to being outsourced than are jobs in other computer specialties because software engineering requires innovation and intense research and development, and database administration often requires immediate responses in real time. If a company's database goes down at 3 P.M., local time, they can't wait for the working day in another country to start before the problem gets fixed.

What's the most important thing someone needs to know when entering the computer industry?
We are all potential users in some form. What I find the most interesting is that in the 70s, early 80s, the enterprise [i.e., large corporations] was driving the computer industry. It was too early in the technology cycle for consumers to have an impact. The advent of the Internet turned this upside down. Computers went from being a closed system to being an open system. Now consumers drive this industry. What they can do with technology in their personal lives (IM, for example, social networking, and accessing search), they expect to be able to do in their corporate lives. That is what is driving the industry.

Oracle Corporation
Oracle Corporation is perhaps best known for its eponymous database management system, but the company also builds tools for database development, middle-tier software, enterprise resource planning software (ERP), customer relationship management software (CRM), and supply chain management (SCM) software. Headquartered in the Bay Area near San Francisco, the company employs an estimated 85,000 people worldwide according to the Oracle Web site. Oracle has earned its place in the computing industry pantheon through organic growth combined with high-profile, well-timed acquisitions, like BEA Systems, Inc. and Hyperion Solutions. Oracle competes for new database licenses on UNIX, Linux, and Windows operating systems primarily against IBM's DB2 and Microsoft SQL Server; however, IBM's DB2 still dominates the mainframe database market. Initially, Oracle was on friendly terms with German

INTERVIEW

Winsome Trading

Darcey Woodard
Computer technician, Redmond, Washington

Can you compare working at a smaller company with working at a larger one?
The first company I worked for was about 100 employees. It was a software company providing financial/payroll/student records services for most schools in Washington state. The next company had just seven IT/programming/support staff. Now, the company I work for probably has about 50 employees, three of whom are in IT, including me.

Do people working at smaller companies often have to play more than one role? What roles naturally go together?
Yes, definitely. Smaller IT staff means [that if] you even look like you are [remotely] familiar with computers, people are going to ask you for help. So even if you are a programmer or a network [administrator], you are going to do hardware support and off-the-shelf software support. And this leads to printer support, which probably leads to phone support, and so on.

In my case, working for smaller companies helped give me a broader scope of skills. At larger companies, you don't get that kind of exposure. You are more pigeonholed. The only thing that will stay the same is the skills your job requires. Larger companies will require you to specialize more in one field [because] there is someone for every position, or multiple people to handle that one position, depending on the company size.

company SAP AG, the world's second largest business software company and the third-largest independent software provider (in terms of revenue), but this cooperation has devolved over the years to an outright rivalry. On March 22, 2007, Oracle sued SAP AG, accusing them of fraud and unfair competition (the case is set to go to trial in February 2010).

Up-and-Coming Players

In March 2009, Gartner Research compiled a list of several vendors to keep an eye on in the coming months for "the way they could aid in cost optimization, operational performance and organizational skill development initiatives." These names encompass a wide variety of segments of the computing industry. For example:

Skytap, a venture-backed company based in Seattle, Washington, provides virtual labs for application development and QA teams. Developers can access these virtual labs and use Skytap's library of prebuilt virtual machine, operating system, and application images; alternatively, they can upload existing virtual machines, builds, or test scripts into the Skytap environment.

LogLogic is a company that enables log data from firewalls, routers, servers, applications, operating systems, and other devices to be automatically collected, stored, reported, and alerted on in near real-time because "bandwidth reduction and greater safeguards against internal and external threats via log management will result in cost savings."

RollStream, Inc. provides a suite of on-demand collaboration tools that allows IT managers to reduce the time and effort required to collaborate and communicate with suppliers or customers on large projects.

NextPlane lets business users communicate through instant messaging and collaborate, regardless of the underlying unified communications platform or service.

G2G3, one of the leading providers of simulation programs, recently partnered with IBM to produce the Virtual Service Management Simulator, an immersive 3D learning system where participants learn how service management and IT infrastructure library (ITIL) processes can be applied to improve business performance.

Big Versus Small

Obviously, many more companies are out there—Amazon, Cisco, Sun Microsystems—a complete analysis of them all is beyond the scope of this book. The point is that some people prefer working for a "big name" company. Take Microsoft, Google, or Sun Microsystems, for example. These companies have instant name-brand recognition, they have a reputation (both good and bad, in all likelihood), and some people like the supposed security that comes with working for a large, well-established company ("supposed" because as of this writing, Microsoft laid off around 5,000 workers in 2009). Other people, however, prefer the challenges that come with working for a smaller company.

Dean Katona is the senior network administrator for Craig McCaw's investment firm, Eagle River Holdings. (Craig McCaw is the founder of McCaw Cellular, now part of AT&T Mobility, and Clearwire Corporation.) He started his career at Microsoft and has moved to smaller and smaller companies over the years, preferring the diversity in job duties. "At my current company (Eagle River), which only has around 70 people," he says, "I wear multiple hats—from network administrator all the way down to help desk. If I don't know something, I need to figure it out or find a resource that can help me figure it out."

Conferences You Can't Afford to Miss

When it comes to conferences, the knowledge you gain there can often give you an edge in advancing your career—not to mention the networking opportunities (among people, that is, not computers!). Looking for conferences you can't afford to miss? Look at key ones that drive technology agendas. For example, VoiceCon. This conference is "designed to help you decide why, when and how to invest in IP telephony, and how to leverage your enterprise communications platform for maximum advantage." Go to conferences aimed at chief technology officers (CTOs), as well as industry-related conferences, such as NetWorld. NetWorld is hosted by Interop, which "is the leading business technology event series. Through in-depth educational programs, workshops, real-world demonstrations...Interop provides the forum for the most powerful innovations and solutions the industry has to offer."

The National Computer Conference is the largest annual computer show in the data processing industry and is sponsored by the American Federation of Information Processing Societies (AFIPS).

CeBIT is the largest technology exposition. Held every year in Hannover, Germany, this trade show "showcases digital IT and telecommunications solutions for home and work environments. The key target groups are users from industry, the wholesale/retail sector, skilled trades, banks, the services sector, government agencies, science and all users passionate about technology." CeBIT is considered the "world's largest and most renowned trade fair for the world of IT and telecommunications."

The Computex trade show in Taipei, Taiwan, is the world's second-largest computer fair behind Germany's enormous CeBIT, with such noteworthy participants as Intel, AMD, ATI, and NVIDIA. The IT industry in Taiwan's IT has become a driving force in the global market. Since many businesses that operate on a global scale have research and deployment centers or production facilities in Taiwan, Computex is one of the key places to discover the latest technologies, developments, and trends.

Interop is "the leading global technology event, with the most comprehensive IT conference and exhibition available. Business and technology leaders attend Interop to get the most up-to-date information available on key technologies, learn about the latest trends and meet with leading vendors."

VoiceCon is a yearly conference with the aim of helping IT professionals build an IP telephony platform that is right for their business and how to leverage it for maximum business advantage. Presentations are conducted by the leading experts, vendors, and enterprise IT executives who will share their knowledge, experience, and expertise.

The Combined Exhibition of Advanced Technologies (CEATEC) is an annual trade show held in October in Makuhari Messe, Japan. Regarded as the Japanese equivalent of Consumer Electronics Show, CEATEC has become Japan's largest IT and electronics exhibition and conference. In 2007, it drew 205,859 people, of which 165,303 were attendees, 38,705 were exhibitors, and 1,851 were press, according to official figures. Such numbers confirmed CEATAC's place as one of the world's largest consumer electronics fairs.

For people specifically interested in Microsoft products, there is TechEd. This conference is aimed at "any and all technology professionals interested in exploring a broad set of current and upcoming Microsoft technologies, tools, platforms, and services." Microsoft also offers conferences on specific products. Organization-wise, there are often user groups where you meet face to face. Following virtual communities via blogs can be good, as long as the author is credible.

Every large company like Microsoft typically has an annual conference, plus some sort of local user community. At the Google I/O Developer Conference, for example, participants will "have a chance to interact directly with the engineering teams who work on our [application programming interfaces] APIs and developer products. [D]ozens of in-depth technical sessions focus on how to write better applications using Google and open technologies." There are sessions and demos for developers who are working on business applications, as well as items of interest for the developer community, such as applications that use the latest Web and mobile technologies. And then there's the Macworld Conference & Expo. Macworld is considered the largest annual Mac gathering in the world, and the most important annual trade exposition for Apple and all Mac hardware and software vendors.

Finally, various computer-related industries often put on conferences. The IEEE, for example, offers workshops, seminars, and conferences throughout the year. Colleges, universities, and technical schools also will have information on upcoming conferences, and counselors or advisors at these schools may even be able to suggest which ones will benefit you the most.

Women in This Industry

This chapter would not be complete without addressing the opportunities for women specifically. According to a 2002 article in the *San Francisco Chronicle*, women make up less than 20 percent of the nation's computer science research graduates. Why is this? Jane Margolis and Allan Fisher, authors of *Unlocking the Clubhouse: Women in Computing* believe they have the answer. "The culture of computer science has been built around male preferences," Fisher said, pointing out how introductory courses in computer science hone in on very technical aspects of the field. Women might also feel more intimidated when they perceive their male counterparts to be more tech-savvy. Margolis said that many female college students interviewed for the book expressed a loss of interest in computer science that really turned out to be a lack of confidence. "Women feel alienated from computers long before they reach college age, and early education should be attentive to their needs," Margolis said.

Anne Moss, senior database administrator at Getty Images, agrees. "A woman in this field needs to be ten times more aggressive than a man," she says. "[Database administration] is still [largely] a man's career, and to succeed, you must be determined, driven, and passionate." Database administration is one of the areas that Anne believes will never get outsourced. "The support needs to be in real-time," she says. "Getty is the leading creator and distributor of still imagery, footage, music, and other content. If a database goes down, it needs to come back up in seconds. That requires immediate access—there's no time to wait for the workday to start in India."

However, this is certainly not the case with all companies. In fact, the size of the company may be a relevant factor. Darcey Woodard, a database applications developer and programmer for Winsome Trading, Inc., has had a different experience in her career. "Maybe it's because [computers] is really a "new" field, so old prejudices weren't as prevalent. Maybe it's because I've only worked in smaller companies...but I also never have had an issue in work-related classes, meetings, etc. Maybe it's because this field is more about being brainy rather than brawny. There are definitely fewer women working in IT, although in the three companies I've worked for, this was not the case. I just saw this whenever I went to talks or workshops or classes." The issue, Darcey believes, is not so much men not respecting women or their abilities. Rather, it's about people in various roles not respecting the jobs of others. Darcey says, "I have had more issues with younger, newer workers not respecting those with experience, hardware guys not respecting programmers, and database administrators not respecting programmers."

Chapter 3

On the Job

When launching a career in the computer industry, it helps to understand the duties and responsibilities of people in key positions. Also, some career paths in this industry are more natural than others. For example, it is more likely for a programmer to become a systems analyst or a database administrator than for a Web designer to follow that career path. And someone working at a smaller company will likely have a different experience than someone who works at a larger company (see chapter 2 for more information about the important differences between small and large companies).

This chapter discusses the key positions in the computing industry. Positions are listed alphabetically within the following categories: programming and software development, information systems operation and management, training and support, Internet and Web site positions, manufacturing, graphics and multimedia, specialist positions, and computer-related office positions. Where possible, opportunities for career advancement are mentioned and connections among positions are provided. In addition, related positions are listed so that areas of crossover may be more readily identified. Additional information can be found in Chapter 6 and in the U.S. Bureau of Labor Statistics *Occupational Outlook Handbook*.

Programming and Software Development

Programmers and developers create software based on certain specifications to solve a particular problem or fulfill a specific need. For example, if a pharmaceutical company needs to track the results of an experimental drug, it is the job of software developers to analyze the problem, write the code, test it, and refine it until the software performs as expected.

Artificial Intelligence Programmer

Artificial intelligence—the field of computer programming that attempts to give machines the ability to reason, think, and learn like humans, using natural language—is a highly interesting, cutting-edge area of computer programming. People in this field design and implement systems that perform complex tasks, such as decision making and recognizing patterns. Practical applications include systems that are used to schedule freight shipments, diagnosing disease, or checking credit; pattern recognition systems that can match faces seen in cameras to a database of criminal or terrorist suspects; and neural network programs that can learn to perform tasks by reevaluating performance. (A neural network is a Web of interconnecting programming constructs that mimic the properties of biological neurons.)

This multidisciplinary field draws on such diverse disciplines as computer science, philosophy, linguistics, and psychology. Some people work purely in a research capacity, creating systems that demonstrate the validity of their theories; others work on a more practical level, using these systems to solve real-world problems. People who enter this field typically start at the intern or trainee level, become a programmer, then a researcher, and then someone who directs artificial intelligence projects. Related fields include data mining, engineering, and systems design.

Bioinformatics Specialist

People in this field typically organize and manipulate information relating to such things as genetic sequences, molecular structures, and other areas of biology. They create and maintain databases of this information and then make them available to biological and medical researchers. One of the more interesting areas has to do with analyzing genetic sequences and predicting their relationship to the structure and function of living things. This is one area where computers are particularly superior to humans—they can calculate in minutes what would take a human years.

Entry-level workers typically start as an associate and move up the ranks to a senior level, finally becoming a director, perhaps of a bioinformatics department or lab. People in this field often find jobs in university laboratories, organizations like the World Health Organization (WHO) or the Centers for Disease Control and Prevention (CDC), or for pharmaceutical companies. Related fields include database analysis, data mining, statistics, and programming.

Computer Programmers

As might be expected, computer programmers write, test, and maintain programs. They also conceive, design, and test programs. Many technical innovations in programming, such as advanced computing technologies and sophisticated new languages and programming tools, have changed the role of a programmer and elevated much of the programming work done today.

Job titles and descriptions can vary, depending on the organization. After software engineers and analysts design software and describe how it will work, the programmer converts that design into a logical series of instructions that the computer can follow. The programmer does this by "translating" the instructions into one of the many programming languages available —the language used depends on the ultimate goal of the program. If you decide to launch a career as a computer programmer, it is best to learn more than one language. This is relatively easy to do since many languages are similar; this will also make you more marketable and valuable as an employee.

Fast Facts

The first computer "programmer" was a woman. Ada Lovelace, the only legitimate child of Lord George Byron, is known today primarily for her description of Charles Babbage's early mechanical general-purpose computer, the analytical engine. Widely considered the "first programmer" since she was writing programs (that is, manipulating symbols according to rules), she also foresaw that computers would go beyond just number-crunching.

Programmers also update, repair, modify, and expand existing programs. Some, especially those working on large projects that involve many programmers, use computer-assisted software engineering (CASE) tools to automate much of the coding process. These tools free up a programmer to concentrate on writing the unique or more challenging parts of a program. Other tools include applications that increase productivity by combining compiling, code walkthrough, code generation, test data generation, and debugging functions. Programmers also use libraries of basic code that can be modified or customized for a specific application. In many cases, several programmers work together as a team under a senior programmer's supervision. It is common for new programmers to work under the supervision of senior programmers, even if they are not working on a huge project.

Programmers test a program by running it to ensure that the instructions are correct and that the program produces the desired outcome. If errors do occur, the programmer must make the appropriate change and recheck the program until it produces the correct results. This process is called testing and debugging, and may continue for as long as a program is used.

Programmers may work directly with experts from various fields to create specialized software—either programs designed for specific clients or packaged software for general use—ranging from games and educational software to programs for desktop publishing and financial planning. Programming of packaged software constitutes one of the hottest segments of the computer programming industry today.

Programmers can be grouped into one of two types: applications programmers and systems programmers. Applications programmers write programs to handle a specific task, such as a program to track inventory within an organization. They also may revise existing packaged software or customize generic applications purchased from vendors. Systems programmers, on the other hand, write programs to maintain and control computer systems software for operating systems, networked systems, and database systems. In some organizations, workers known as programmer-analysts are responsible for both systems analysis and programming.

Database Analyst

A database analyst designs and creates programs used to collect, maintain, and analyze data used by business organizations, government entities, and other institutions, and runs related reports that managers and analysts then use when making business decisions. In addition, a database analyst changes these programs to reflect changes in business practices, new standards, or new regulations. A person in this field typically starts at the trainee level, becomes an analyst, then a database administrator, and then an information systems manager. Related fields include systems analysis, Web design, and data mining.

Data Miner

Data miners study databases in a wide range of areas—business, government, science—and study the information these databases contain, applying certain tools and algorithms to them and looking for patterns that can leverage these databases. For example, online stores typically recommend additional purchases based on recent selections. This is an example of data mining. Most entry-level workers start as a database analyst or junior-level specialist, becoming a data mining specialist, then a senior consultant or project leader, and then a director or executive in a laboratory or corporation, for example. Related fields include programming, bioinformatics, statistics, systems analysis, database analysis, database administrator, and artificial intelligence.

Program Manager

In terms of the computer industry, this position typically has an emphasis in software development, and a program manager is responsible for overseeing all aspects of a development project, assigns tasks, manages schedules, and coordinates efforts of developers, programmers, testers, and more. They typically work for companies that produce commercial software, and often move into upper levels of management. Projects managers often work closely with people in marketing or sales, since the successful launch of a product is often contingent upon all the pieces coming together at the right time. The typical career path for a program manager is information systems manager and then chief information officer (CIO). Related fields include systems analysis and marketing.

Scientific or Engineering Programmer

Programmers in this area work closely with scientists and engineers to define problems and provide programs that can simulate, for example, natural phenomena or experimental results, so that scientists and engineers can analyze theories and see how certain variables affect outcomes. Scientific/engineering programmers often work in research laboratories or manufacturing facilities, as well as biotech, chemical, and aviation firms. Most entry-level programmers advance to the senior level and then become a project manager. Related fields include robotic engineering, systems programming, bioinformatics, data mining, and statistics.

Software Engineer

Computer software engineers apply the principles of computer science and mathematical analysis to the design, development, testing, and evaluation of the software and systems that make computers work. The tasks performed by these workers change rapidly, reflecting new areas of specialization or changes in technology, as well as the unique needs of their employers.

Software engineers can be involved in the design and development of many types of software, including computer games, word processing and business applications, operating systems and network distribution, and compilers, which convert programs to machine language for execution on a computer.

Similar to systems analysts, computer software engineers begin by analyzing users' needs, and then design, test, and develop software to meet those needs. They may also take on the role of a computer programmer but not always. Computer software engineers must be experts in operating systems and middleware (software that acts as a bridge between software programs or applications) to ensure that the underlying systems will work properly.

Examples of duties a software engineer may be responsible for include tracking each department's computer needs for a company—ordering, inventory, billing, and payroll, for example—and making suggestions about the technical direction. They also might set up the organization's intranets—networks that link computers within the organization and ease communication among various departments.

People in this field often start as a software engineer or programmer or analysts, move to a lead programmer or systems analyst, then into project management, and then to managing information systems. Related fields include systems programming, database analysis, data mining, and systems integration.

Systems Analyst

A systems analyst, as the name implies, analyzes an organization's needs and designs programs to meet these needs. This includes writing the "blueprints" for the software program, choosing the most appropriate tools and methods, supervising the writing of the code, testing the program, fixing bugs, and adding requested features. Such people often work with both technical and nontechnical staff.

As a systems analyst gains experience, he or she may be promoted to senior or lead positions, or even into management positions, such as manager of information systems or chief information officer. Those who find their career leads them into a particular niche may find opportunities as independent consultants, or may choose to start their own consulting firms. Related fields include system integration, database analysis, and information systems manager.

Systems Consultant

Similar to a systems analyst, a systems consultant analyzes problems and designs appropriate solutions, with an emphasis on selecting, installing, and configuring hardware and software. Because this person is often brought in to a company on a short-term basis, they may also have a hand in training employees in the operation of a new system. Their services are typically required when a company is expanding its information processing facilities or experiencing problems integrating systems and software. Because systems consultants work in a short-term or freelance capacity, the career path is typically what such a person creates for him- or herself. Some do go on to become information systems managers at a company. Related fields include systems analysis and systems integration.

Systems Programmer

A systems programmer, unlike an applications programmer, for example, builds the tools that other programmers use. They design and write programs that interact with a computer's low-level operating system, such as device drivers and utilities. Some work directly on the development of operating systems; others write drivers (special programs that allow an operating system to control peripheral devices like printers and mice); still others write development aids that programmers use to write code, such as compilers and editors. In most cases, a systems programmer starts out in an entry-level position, is promoted to a senior-level position, and then becomes a lead programmer or project manager in systems development. Related fields include user interface design and systems design.

User Interface Designer

This person designs the menus, icons, graphics, and other features that people use when interacting with a computer program or operating system (called a graphical user interface, or GUI). When carrying out this task, a user interface designer looks to make the interface components intuitive, consistent, and not awkward. For example, it makes sense to use an icon that looks like a trash can to indicate where to send a deleted folder, or a pencil icon to indicate a word-processing program. In addition, components and techniques should be the same across applications in a suite (cutting and pasting, for example, should be the same in Microsoft Word as it is in Microsoft Excel).

In most cases, people in this field start at the trainee level, become an actual user interface designer, than a lead designer, and then a manager. Related fields include technical writing, systems analysis, systems programming and integration, and multimedia.

Information Systems Operation and Management

Computer systems are complex, and becoming even more so as more uses for which the computer can be applied emerge. In addition, computer networks change rapidly and require round-the-clock maintenance and troubleshooting. People in this field operate, test, manage, and support computer systems and networks.

Chief Information Officer

This is typically the highest-ranking information services executive in a company. This person is responsible for long-term planning and organization-wide policy with respect to all computer-related activities. They often present proposals to the chief executive officer (CEO) or to a corporation's board of directors. A CIO pays attention to how their competitors are using technology and how their company can use it better. Since this is a top-level executive position, any moves from here are typically in a lateral direction, such as chief executive officer or vice president for research or planning.

Chief Technology Officer

This position is similar in duties and scope to a chief information officer and is a high-level position responsible for leveraging monetary, intellectual, or political capital into technology to further a company's objectives or goals. They often oversee technical staff, particularly those engaged in the development of new technologies or in software development. Whereas a chief information officer is focused on solving problems or meeting the company's goals by using existing technology, the chief technology officer is looking to achieve these same things by developing new technologies. As with a CIO, this is a top-level executive position, so career moves will go in a lateral rather than vertical direction.

Computer Security Specialist

This person is responsible for protecting computer systems against all forms of illegal intrusion, including viruses, data theft, fraud, and more. This can be achieved by setting up automatic security monitoring programs, reviewing system logs for evidence of tampering, and educating users about the importance of good security practices (some feel this is the hardest part of the job!), among other things. In most companies, a person in this line of works starts at the trainee or assistant level, becomes a security specialist, and then is promoted to director of information systems security. Related fields include technical writing, technical support, systems design, programming, and artificial intelligence.

Database Administrator

Database administrators work with database management systems software and determine ways to organize and store data. They identify user needs and set up new computer databases. In many cases, database administrators must integrate data from outdated systems into a new one. They also test and coordinate modifications to the system when needed and troubleshoot problems when they occur. This person ensures the performance of the system, understands the platform on which the database runs, and adds new users to the system. Because many databases are connected to the Internet, database administrators also must plan and coordinate security measures with network administrators. With the growing volume of sensitive data and the increasing interconnectedness of computer networks, data integrity, backup systems, and database security have become increasingly important aspects of the job of database administrators.

Database administrators typically begin their careers as database analysts or programmers, then move into administration, then information systems management, eventually becoming a chief information officer (CIO). Related fields include systems administration, database analysis, Internet applications programmer, and Web design.

Information Systems Auditor

Auditors of electronic data processing (EDP) keep a close eye on data processing applications, looking for errors and mistakes—both accidental and cases of fraud. These people may also be responsible for ensuring that the companies they work for adhere to certain government regulations and industry standards. Such jobs are often in high demand in industries such as banking, insurance, and accounting, where there is a large amount of financial data and its proper handling must be safeguarded. People in this field typically start at a trainee- or entry-level position and are promoted through the ranks, eventually reaching a senior-level position. Some go on to become a partner at a public accounting firm, become freelance consultants, or manage an auditing department in a company. Related fields include systems analyst, certified public accountant (CPA), and computer security.

Information Systems Director

This is the person in charge of planning for and supervising all information systems departments in an organization. This includes developing IT-related budgets, expansion plans, strategic plans, and more. They often work with managers in other departments to set organization-wide standards with regard to equipment, training, and other practices, as well as to devise ways of using computer technology to provide better service and better meet the company's goals. People in this position typically start as a systems administrator, become a low-level manager in a related department (such as data processing), and then become a director of information systems. In small to medium-sized companies, this position may be at

Everyone

Knows

By far, the most common PC myths concern viruses. Novice computer users are renowned for assuming that anything that goes wrong with their PC must be caused by a virus, and misguided virus warnings are one of the most popular kinds of non-commercial junk e-mail. While it is possible for a piece of e-mail to become harmful because programs like Microsoft Outlook have more complex abilities than they used to, "pseudo-viruses" are more common. Part virus and part Trojan horse, these entities look like something harmless—for example, an e-mail with an attached text or a movie file—but once they have been released onto a user's computer, they can wreak all kinds of havoc. (These items have to be specifically executed before they do anything.)

Avoiding viruses is simple. Use virus-checker software, and keep it updated. Do not run mysterious programs sent to you by e-mail. Look carefully at attached files to make sure that they are not called something like foo.txt.vbs (this indicates a Visual Basic script file, not a text file). Do not run macros in unknown documents in programs like Microsoft's Office suite.

If you've received a questionable virus warning, or if you just want to know how to spot them, the Vmyths.com Web site is the place to go. For information on what viruses really do exist, start at Virus Bulletin, a highly regarded source of information on viruses.

the top level. In larger companies, an information systems director may go on to become chief information officer. Related fields include systems administration, computer operations, technical support, and management.

Information Systems Manager

This position is often one step below that of information systems director at many companies. Duties typically include overseeing all aspects of information technology operation, such as technical support, training, network administration, and database operations. They may work for universities, government offices, or small to medium-sized companies. Specific responsibilities may include supervising system administrators, preparing operating budgets, and planning for the upgrading or expansion of software. Information systems managers often work with managers in other departments to ensure appropriate and efficient use of computer resources and to make sure that users' needs and questions are met. People in this position typically start as a systems administrator or support manager or support technician. From here, an information systems manager can move into a director position or even chief information officer. Related fields include systems administrator, systems analyst, and systems consultant.

Network/Systems Administrator

Network/systems administrators and data communications analysts, also referred to as network architects, design, test, and evaluate systems such as local area networks (LANs), wide area networks (WANs), the Internet, intranets, and other data communications systems. Systems are configured in many ways and can range from a connection between two offices in the same building to globally distributed networks, voice mail, and e-mail systems of a multinational organization. Network/systems administrators perform network modeling, analysis, and planning, often requiring both hardware and software solutions. For example, a network may involve the installation of several pieces of hardware, such as routers and hubs, wireless adaptors, and cables, while also requiring the installation and configuration of software, such as network drivers. Analysts also may research related products and make necessary hardware and software recommendations. Systems and network administrators often become information systems managers. Related fields include systems analysis, programming, software engineer, technical support, and technical writing.

Quality Assurance Specialist

A quality assurance (QA) specialist is responsible for testing and evaluating software programs to make sure they work correctly and meet the required specifications. They support programmers, who are focused more on the inner workings of a program and who do not always anticipate ways in which users will actually use a program.

In a sense, programmers are depending on QA specialists to find the bugs they missed. These people may also suggest ways a particular software program can be improved. QA specialists often start at a trainee level and then become a specialist. The more experienced specialists are promoted to a senior-level position. This person could be someone who has crossed over from a technical support or help-desk job. Other related fields include technical writer, tester, and user interface design.

Training and Support

Because computer applications, software packages, operating systems, and so on are so complex—and because they seem to be changing constantly—there is a need for people to help the users of such products. A trainer may be called in when a company switches to a new operating system, for example, or when a new database program is installed. Trainers teach the users how to use the product, often including information on helpful shortcuts and how to use the product most efficiently. Once the trainer's job is done, however, problems may still emerge. That's where the support person comes in. Support specialists help users answer specific questions and solve particular problems. For example, if a user of an e-mail and calendaring system is having trouble sending and receiving e-mail, the technical support person will walk him or her through the solution, sticking with the problem until it is resolved.

Technical Support Specialist

Help-desk technicians typically work with external user. Technical support specialists, however, are generally in-house in that they respond to inquiries from their organizations' computer users and may run automatic diagnostics programs to resolve problems. They also install, modify, clean, and repair computer hardware and software. They may write training manuals and train users in how to use new computer hardware and software. These people also oversee the daily performance of their company's computer systems and evaluate how useful software programs are. As with help-desk technicians, people in this field often start at an entry level, work up to the senior level, and then go into a management position. Related fields include testing, systems consultant, technical writer, and technical editor.

Technical Support Manager

This person may oversee either a help-desk department or an internal technical support department. Duties typically include hiring and training support technicians, coordinating shift schedules, assembling and organizing support documentation (such as manuals or databases), and providing supplementary support or resolving escalated situations. Technical support managers often work with engineers, program developers, and technical writers to resolve problems with a software program or to improve its usability. People in this field typically have moved up the ranks to become a senior technical support representative or a shift manager at a help desk. From a management position, they may advance to a director of technical support, depending on the size of the organization. Related fields include technical editing, technical writing, information systems manager, and systems administration.

Service Technician

Sooner or later, it happens: a hard drive crashes, a monitor no longer displays properly, or a computer in general is just not behaving the way it should. That's when the service technician comes in. Duties include (among other things) installing and testing new computers, repairing and upgrading equipment, and running diagnostic programs to determine the source of a problem. Some large companies have in-house technicians; most work for computer manufacturers or computer stores, supporting the products they sell. People who follow this career path and establish a good service record find themselves promoted to a senior-level position and perhaps eventually managing a service department. Related fields include computer hardware manufacturing technician, systems integration, technical support, and sales.

Software Applications Trainer

People who have an in-depth understanding of certain software programs may find it rewarding to teach others. Trainers usually offer classes in specific programs or operating systems, and can work within corporations, community colleges, vocational schools, employment agencies, adult education, or continuing education centers. Such positions are often in constant demand—software is always being updated and workers need retraining when previous skills fall by the wayside. People typically enter this field as a basic or entry-level instructor. As they gain experience, they often advance to become a senior-level trainer, a manager in charge of other trainers, or an independent consultant, offering advanced or specialized workshops. Related positions include technical writing, technical support, and management.

Technical Writer

Technical writers create a wide range of materials: books, manuals, documents, online help systems, tutorials, reference books, and more. They are also responsible for writing text that appears within a user interface—tooltips, for example, or the text that appears in pop-up messages or dialog boxes. They can work for trade publishers, software companies, information technology departments, or independently. If they work for a software company, they often have to work with the development team and programmers, staying in the loop about how a program is supposed to work, what its features are, how they can best meet users' needs, and so on. Technical writers who work on a freelance basis can take their career in nearly any direction they choose, provided they are motivated and self-disciplined enough. Technical writers working for a company may advance to a position where they are a lead writer, supervising other writers, or even to manager of a publications department. Related fields include technical editing, Web site design, and desktop publisher.

Technical Editor

Technical editors are responsible for ensuring the accuracy of technical writing. This may include basic copyediting skills, like checking grammar, spelling, and punctuation, but also can include ensuring that the material the writer has produced is well organized, easy to understand, accurate, and thorough. Most of the time, technical editors work closely with technical writers, but they can also work with developers, programmers, and project managers. They also work with the graphics or production departments to make sure that screen images and diagrams are laid out properly. Technical editors can work in a freelance capacity, which is often the case with software publishers or trade publishers, or they may work for a publications department in a specific company. Someone seeking to become a technical editor may start with a company as an editorial assistant first, then advance to become a senior-level editor, and then from there into management. Managing editors who work for a computer book publisher often worked first as a technical editor. Related fields include technical writing, multimedia development, Web site design, and project management.

Telecommunications Technician/Engineer

These are the people responsible for physically setting up computer systems, including the cables, telephone, or fiber-optic lines used for networking and communication; troubleshooting any problems that may arise; and configuring, specifying, and monitoring the configuration and transmission of data, among other things. When entering this field, people typically do so at the trainee or assistant level and then move up to a senior position. From there, depending on the size of the company, they may move into a supervisory or managerial positions. Some go on to pursue careers in engineering. Related fields include network analysis, computer hardware technician, hardware manufacturing, and service technician.

Internet and Web Site Positions

While the dot-com boom busted a while back, there is no denying that the Internet has changed forever the way the world does business, how we communicate and stay in touch, how we obtain information, and how students learn (for example, today, it's possible to obtain a degree online without ever setting foot inside a classroom). In addition, more areas are moving from their traditional presence or medium to the Web—consider that many major newspapers and magazines have stopped producing a print version and have moved their operations online, among them the *Seattle Post-Intelligencer*, the *Cincinnati Post*, the *Christian Science Monitor*, and *PC Magazine*.

Internet Advertising Designer

Advertising is a huge, nearly inescapable, fact of life on the Internet. From pop-up ads to banner ads to sponsored links to programs like Google's AdWords, people who understand this new frontier of

Best ▸
Practice

For those people who don't think computer security is really all that important, consider the following:

According to a November 2006 article in *Nucleus Research and KnowledgeStorm*, one in three workers write down their computer password, undermining their security.

According to a September 2006 survey in *Consumer Reports*, roughly one in three computer users has been a victim of viruses, spyware, or phishing. U.S. consumers spent $7.8 billion from 2004 to 2006 on computer repairs, parts, and replacements because of malware attacks.

In March 2006, the Enterprise Strategy Group reported that 68 percent of information security professionals at large organizations say laptops pose the biggest security risk.

Security is a big deal. Passwords need to be strong, meaning they can't easily be figured out; all computing equipment needs to be secure at all times; and any suspicious e-mails, pop-up messages, or other activity should be reported immediately. The computer security specialist's job should be made easier by employees, not harder!

advertising and can grab the attention of someone surfing the Web can do well for themselves. Internet advertising designers, like their traditional print counterparts, are responsible for creating effective advertising for Web sites, often combining text, animation, and sound. Because Internet advertising designers need to know how effective their ads are, they often work closely with other members of the marketing department, Web site designers, and programmers. People in this field may start out in graphic design and eventually into management, or may find more success working in a freelance capacity. Related fields include Web site design, applications programming, and technical writing.

Internet Applications Programmer

An Internet applications programmer, while a programmer at heart, is focused more on developing programs that add features and functionalities to a Web site, such as animations, forms, and shopping carts. Life is moving more and more onto the Internet—both business life and home life—and people are turning to the Internet as a source of entertainment, shopping, games, information, and more. Responsibilities of an Internet applications programmer can include writing programs for Web browsers, search engines, e-commerce, chat programs, and video conferencing. Unlike traditional programmers, Internet applications programmers do not usually use languages like C++. Rather, they use languages like Java, JavaScript, or VBScript. They are also highly proficient in Hypertext Markup Language (HTML).

Internet applications programmers often work with advertising and marketing departments, and may also work with writers and editors on occasion. Related fields include Web site design, computer graphics, animation/special effects programmer, and multimedia development.

Internet Service Provider

This term refers to a business entity that provides home and business customers an account through which they access the Internet. This often includes space for a Web site, hosting, and related services. Internet service providers (ISPs) connect to the Internet through special, high-capacity phone lines and arrange connections to nearby Internet "backbones"—larger ISPs that agree to pass their traffic through. Duties include setting up accounts and providing technical support for customers, and monitoring local connections and creating alternate routes, if need be. The prospects for small to medium-sized ISPs are not great, given the larger competition presented by companies like America Online, EarthLink, Verizon, and the like. Most people in this field work for the larger companies. A person typically enters this field at an entry-level support position and from there goes into management or a director position. Related fields include Web site design, Internet applications programmer, and Internet advertising designer.

Internet Store Manager/Entrepreneur

Perhaps the best example of this is Amazon.com) or eBay; however, individuals can set up and run a business on the Internet, too—sometimes with a great deal of success! Someone who is considering this endeavor certainly has a lot of responsibility, just like any other business owner. They are responsible for handling all aspects of the business: accounts receivable, accounts payable, shipping, invoicing, ordering product (if necessary), and more. Furthermore, this person is responsible for designing the Web site, as well as marketing and advertising. The fortunate entrepreneur who is just starting out may have the funds to hire people to do these tasks, but this isn't typically the case. People who are successful in this field may expand the services or goods offered, or may collaborate with other businesses or Internet service providers. Related fields include interactive advertising designer, sales, and computer programming (knowledge of HTML is helpful).

Webmaster

To be sure, Web site designers can play a role in maintaining and updating a Web site, but that type of oversight often falls to the Webmaster. This person may oversee writers and programmers who provide content for the site, monitor the site's performance, and ensure its security. Webmasters typically begin their career as a Web site designer, then go into applications programming, eventually becoming a Webmaster. In smaller companies, this job may just be one of many the default "techie" is responsible for. In a larger company, however, a dedicated Webmaster is required. Related fields include Internet applications programmer, systems/network administration, and multimedia.

Web Site Designer

A Web designer—also called a Web programmer, Web developer, Internet or intranet developer, or Webmaster— is responsible for day-to-day Web site creation and design. Web designers combine the skills of a computer programmer with those of a graphic designer. They work with all of the elements of a Web site—text, images, graphics, and more—to come up with functional, interesting, and user-friendly designs.

Because this is still a relatively new position as far as computer technology goes, there is no real path for advancement, per se. As with consultants, this position often evolves into whatever the motivated person wants it to be. As skills grow, so, too, can responsibilities. There can be crossover between Web site design and applications programming, so a person who is looking to advance his or her career as a Web site designer would do well to acquire knowledge of programming. Other related fields include systems/network administrator, multimedia developer, technical writing, and technical editing.

Manufacturing

Gone are the days when humans spent their working hours in an assembly line—today, these humans have robot workers to do their job. Computers play a huge role in manufacturing—whether it's a database system to track shipments and inventory or a simulation that allows engineers to test a particular design before spending time and resources constructing it, only to discover a hidden flaw.

Computer-aided Design Technician/Manager

Computer-aided design (CAD) is a software program used by engineers and designers to create detailed design drawings, with information on specifications, cost, dimensions, part numbers, and more. These software programs enable CAD technicians to easily make changes to plans, as well as shift or rotate them on the virtual page, which provides better visualization of a product's structure and function, for example. These technicians often work in the automotive, architecture, electronic, mechanical engineering, and other industries. People in this field typically start at an assistant-level or drafter position and are promoted to a senior-level position, eventually becoming a manager of a CAD team or another management position. Related fields include technical writing, technical editing, hardware design, and systems design.

Computer-aided Manufacturing Technician

While a CAD technician has to do with design, the computer-aided manufacturing (CAM) technician focuses on the production of items. For example, a CAM technician may work in an automobile plant, where computer-controlled machines perform the assembly line tasks that used to be done by human workers. Regardless of what is being produced, CAM technicians are primarily responsible for setting up and maintaining the machines that automate this process. Because this involves an intricate understanding of all the components—size, shape, measurements, pieces, placement, and other characteristics—CAM technicians often work closely with members in other departments, such as architects, managers, drafters, and programmers. People entering this field typically do so at a trainee level and then move up the ranks to become a senior or lead technician. From there, a management position in either a CAD or CAM department is certainly an option. Alternatively, some CAM technicians go on to become engineers. Related fields include CAD, engineering, and hardware design.

Computer Hardware Designer/Engineer

These designers and engineers are responsible for producing central processing units (CPUs), memory chips, circuitry, and other computer components. They may work with software programmers and testers in order to make their products more efficient. A career path in this area typically starts at an entry-level position, and then advances to a senior-level status, eventually becoming a lead engineer. Or, this person may choose to become a department manager or project manager. Related fields include embedded systems design and robotics engineering.

Computer Hardware Manufacturing Technician

These technicians often work under designers and engineers, testing the designs or hardware components, making sure they work as intended and that there are no unforeseen problems. Often, this involves actually building the components they are testing. People in this field generally start in an assistant-level position, performing routine tests. As experience and proficiency is gained, someone in this field can expect to advance to a senior or supervisory position. Alternatively, a person may make the switch to engineering. Related fields include service technician, technical support, hardware manufacturing and design, engineering, and systems integration.

Computer Systems Designer

Any computer system that is available online or in a store was carefully created and designed by a computer systems designer. These designers select each separate component—the disk drives, motherboard, video system, etc.—to put together systems designed for specific users and their needs. For example, the average home computer user will have different requirements than someone who is

On the Cutting Edge

Ever feel like you're going through ink cartridges faster than you can replace them—and that those cartridges cost more than the printer itself? Zink Imaging may have the answer. A technology that was begun at Polaroid and perfected by Zink, inkless photo printing uses millions of colorless dye crystals layered under polymer-coated paper. When the crystals are heated at different temperatures at specific intervals, they melt onto the paper in the traditional cyan, magenta, yellow, and black used by inkjet, laser, and other printing devices. While the technology isn't likely to replace the standard desktop or network printer anytime soon, what it does do, according to Zink's chief marketing officer Scott Wicker, is "enable printing where it doesn't currently exist ... without the need for ink cartridges or ribbons, printers can now be built into small, mobile devices such as digital cameras."

purchasing a "fleet" of computers for a business—a system for a home user may have a decent graphics and sound systems (since many people use their computer to play games), whereas a business user's computer may have a more powerful processor to keep up with data processing and storage demands.

People often begin in an entry-level position, are eventually promoted to a senior-level position, and then become a lead designer or move into management. Others may prefer to become a consultant for other companies. Systems designers often work closely with people in the marketing department and with programmers. Related fields include systems integration, computer hardware design and engineering, telecommunications, embedded systems design, and technical support.

Embedded Systems Designer

An embedded computer system can be thought of as a "hidden" computer. For example, a handheld gaming device, an electronic scanner, even a phone are all considered specialized computers. And an embedded systems designer is the person responsible for conceiving and designing such systems. They often work with other designers and engineers and may also work with people in the marketing department. As with most other areas discussed in this chapter, advancement typically moves from an entry-level position, then to a senior level, and then to management. Related fields include robotics, hardware engineering and design, telecommunications, and computer-aided manufacturing.

Robotics Engineer/Technician

People in this field are responsible for designing and implementing robots (or robotic systems) for use in such wide-ranging areas as manufacturing, research, or service. (Service robots are not in a fixed position, as in an assembly line; rather, they move around a factory or hospital, for example, delivering goods. Another great example of a service robot is that used by bomb squads or fire departments.) This is a comprehensive field—robotics engineers and technicians combine electronics, engineering, AI, computer science, and more to design and test these robots. Engineers and technicians can work in manufacturing, universities, government organizations, or industrial laboratories. As with many other positions discussed in this chapter, people often begin in an entry-level position, are eventually promoted to a senior-level position, and then become a lead engineer or move into management. Others may find success branching off on their own as a consultant for other companies. Related fields include AI programming, computer-aided design and manufacturing, and engineering.

Graphics and Multimedia

Whether used in a video game, a Web site, or an educational program, graphics, sound, music, narration, and more play an extensive role in many computer-related areas. For example, consider an online training demo that shows the user exactly how to create a slideshow presentation, including how to add interesting effects to the text, how to add a soundtrack, and how transitions between slides should look.

Animation/Special Effects Programmer

As the title implies, an animation/special effects programmer is responsible for creating the sequences of images (often quite lifelike) used in computer games, multimedia presentations, and more. Such programmers often have a strong background in art as well as computers. People in this field typically begin as an entry-level animator, then become a programmer, then advance to a senior-level position, and perhaps becoming a director or manager of a multimedia department. Related fields include programming and multimedia development.

Computer Game Designer/Programmer

As one might expect, this person is responsible for designing and creating programs for computer games, whether it's a role-playing game, arcade-style game, strategy game, or simulation. They often work with writers, editors, electronic sound producers, programmers, and special effects producers. A person entering this field typically does so as an assistant programmer or coder, eventually becoming a bona fide designer or developer, and then becoming a lead developer or project manager. Some people also see success working in a freelance capacity, but must have an established reputation first. Related fields include testing and multimedia development.

Computer Graphic Artist

This person designed computer-generated art or images for a multitude of purposes: Web sites, computer games, multimedia presentations, and more. When entering this field, a person may start as a technician, doing routine work scanning, manipulating, and otherwise working with graphics images, including digital photos. As skills are acquired and techniques refined, a person will move from graphics artist/designer to perhaps the director of an art department in a company. Related fields include computer game design and programming.

Electronic Sound Producer

This is the person responsible for the auditory components of a computer game or multimedia presentation. Such people may use live recording, sound archives, synthesized music, and more when creating sound effects. Advancement in this field generally is linear, from entry-level to senior-level positions. At a high level, some producers manage engineers and technicians. Others may go on to become director of an art department or even become a consultant. Related fields include computer game design, animation, graphics, and multimedia development.

Multimedia Developer/Producer

These are the people responsible for designing and programming—and in some cases overseeing—interactive multimedia projects. As the name implies, multimedia refers to something that combines audio, images, and text. Consider an interactive encyclopedia, for example. There is the text of the articles, the pictures of the subjects, and perhaps a short video showing how something works. Just as with most career paths, people in this field typically start in an entry-level position, perhaps as an assistant, and move up through the ranks, from lead developer to producer, and then into a director or other management position. Some people also experience success working in a freelance capacity, but must have established a proven track record first. Related fields include Web site design, software applications, multimedia, and project management.

Multimedia or Game Writer/Editor

These are the people who write and edit the text that accompanies multimedia presentations or games. This can include a wide range of items, including articles, instructions, scripts, and descriptions, among other things. They often work with graphic artists, animators, programmers, and sound or special effects producers. People do not often enter this field as a writer. They typically start as an editorial assistant or some other position and then take advantage of writing opportunities as they arise until they are promoted to an actual position as writer or editor. From there, they may become a project editor or manager. Writers who establish especially noteworthy reputations may find success as a freelancer. Related fields include technical writing and editing.

Virtual Reality Designer/Programmer

Virtual reality—a simulated version of the world we experience around us, including sights, sounds, and sensations—is an intriguing aspect of computer science. Developers and programmers who choose to focus on this area may help develop games, virtual tours of museums or other historical sites (past and present), or simulations for people like astronauts and airline pilots. They typically work with researchers, other programmers and developers, and engineers. Unlike many of the other positions discussed in this chapter, there is not a real career ladder, per se, in virtual reality. Naturally, it is possible to become promoted into a senior or lead position; however, from there, people often move into the academic world, becoming a professor or working in research. Related fields include computer game design and programming and graphics.

Specialist Positions

While some people work in the computer industry proper, perhaps as a programmer, a Webmaster, a network administrator, there are those who work in the industry more broadly. These are the people who monitor the industry as a whole, those who sell the products the rest of the world uses, those who market those products, and those who study the industry carefully, looking for trends and (hopefully) making accurate predictions.

Industry Analyst

People who are able to follow—and perhaps even anticipate—trends in the computing industry are valuable indeed, as in any field. Because this particular field changes so fast, however, people who have special insight and who can analyze performance among companies may find themselves of special importance to those working in product development or marketing. Analysts who focus on the computer industry compile information on both the big picture and the little picture: How are specific companies doing? What effect is that having on the industry as a whole? What sectors or particular stocks should a company invest in? Where are the problem areas, and what companies or trends should be avoided? It's the job of the analyst to answer these and other questions. Some work in-house for companies, some work for business publications, and others work in the investment industry. Analysts often work with marketing and accounting departments, as well as with upper-level managers. When working for a particular company, a person typically starts at the assistant level, works up to a senior-level position, and perhaps becomes a manager of an investment research group. People who are deemed to have particular, valuable knowledge—the pundit—may even find themselves a regular guest on news programs. Related fields include marketing, journalism, and public relations.

Marketing Specialist

Just as with any field, people who choose to focus on marketing become a knowledgeable expert in a given domain—in this case, computers (this can include everything from software to hardware and anything in between). Marketing specialists study this industry, identifying possible new markets; creating brochures and other display material; performing demonstrations at trade shows and conferences; and using surveys, focus groups, and other forms of feedback to determine if customers' needs are being met and how a product or service can be improved. People generally enter this field as an assistant, become a specialist or focus on research, then become an assistant marketing manager or product manager, before becoming the manager of a marketing department. Related fields include project management, research, and consulting.

Sales Representatives/Managers

Although they often promote a particular product line, the most successful salespeople help customers select the items (hardware, software, peripherals, or all three) that best meet their needs. Clients can range from individual users to corporations to schools to libraries and beyond. People typically start out at the entry level in sales, working as an associate, then as a representative, and then as a manager. Local managers can go on to become district, regional, and then national managers. Related fields include advertising and marketing.

Computer-Related Office Positions

Not every job in the field of computers and programming is *in* the field, per se. Yet, it is difficult—if not impossible—to find an industry, or any job, for that matter, where computers aren't used in some form. Even the coffee stand on the corner uses a computer system to ring up drink sales and track frequent-buyer purchases. Jobs in this category may be traditional paper-based jobs that have moved to computers, such as typing or accounting (now performed with word-processing and spreadsheet applications, respectively).

Data Entry Operator

This position is exactly what it sounds like—entering data into a computer system. This can be data from bank statements, data for an online application, or data for an online survey. However, this job is not always as easy as it sounds. The data must be entered accurately and as error-free as possible and performed at a steady, efficient pace. People often start at an entry-level position and move up the ladder into more senior positions, perhaps becoming an office manager or the manager of a data entry department (this is more often the case with larger companies). Related fields include desktop publishing, word processing, and typesetting.

Desktop Publisher

A desktop publisher is responsible for designing, creating, and laying out all sorts of documents, including fact sheets, brochures, pamphlets, magazines, books, and everything in between. While they often work with writers and editors, some desktop publishers take these tasks on themselves. Many desktop publishers work in a freelance capacity. Others work in print shops or production departments of publishers, advertising agencies, or public relations firms. When working for a particular company, a person may start out as an assistant and move up as they gain experience, eventually managing a publications department, for example. Related fields include word processing, technical writing and editing, Web site design, and multimedia development.

Statistician

Like an industry analyst, statisticians also analyze data and draw conclusions from it. Unlike analysts, however, statisticians focus on mathematical data, using it to create computer simulations, which can then be compared to real-world scenarios. People entering this field typically start as an assistant. As they gain experience, they can be promoted to a senior level, and may even become director of a statistical research department or move into academia. Related fields include accounting, database analysis, data mining, engineering, programming, and marketing.

Systems Integrator

This person is responsible for combining various hardware and software components into a system that best meets a particular client's needs (typically, these clients are large companies with anywhere from dozens to hundred of users). A systems integrator achieves this task by becoming familiar with the company—the physical location, what kind of business the company is engaged in, and how it carries out this business. Once the recommendations have been made and approved, the systems integrator oversees its installation, which can include training workers, if needed, and monitoring the system for a time, fixing any problems or issues that come up. People entering this field may start in a company and eventually become an independent consultant, or they may start as a technical assistant, gain experience as a systems integrator, and then become a systems engineer. Related fields include systems analysis and sales.

Chapter 4

Tips for Success

You have your foot in the door in the computer industry. How do you keep your career on track? How is this track even determined? What are the best ways to advance in this career? What are the quickest ways to undermine that career?

This chapter will address these questions with specific tips and techniques, including what certifications and degrees are recommended, what qualities set candidates apart, and more. Industry veterans will also provide advice on how to establish a professional reputation—and things that can ruin it. The first part of this chapter provides tips for success relating to specific positions. These pointers can be applied to similar occupations. Tips for an occupation that is not specifically mentioned here can be extrapolated by looking at a related position. For example, someone who works as a system consultant may find the tips given for a software programmer to be equally valuable.

In addition, people often do not stay in the position or group that they begin their career in. With the computing industry, changing jobs is often an important way of furthering one's career. This makes sense when you consider the importance of staying abreast of the technology, anticipating changes and trends where possible, and moving to take advantage of them. The same experience, credentials, and traits that will help you advance your career by getting a job at a different company also are likely to help you get promoted within a company.

Computer Programmers

A bachelor's degree typically is required for computer programming jobs, although a two-year degree or certificate may be adequate for some positions, depending on the size of the company. Employers typically favor applicants who already have relevant programming skills and experience, but that does not mean you cannot take a different job at a company to get your foot in the door and move up from there. As your career progresses, skilled programmers who keep up-to-date with the latest technology usually have good opportunities for advancement. However, don't jump on the latest trend or fad in programming just because it's currently hot. Make sure it aligns with your career goals.

Best Practice

In order to get the most out of your career and see it truly move forward, consider the following advice from Rob Short: "Make sure each assignment has something new in it. You want five years of experience, not one year of experience five times."

Some computer programmers have a college degree in computer science, mathematics, or information systems; others have taken special courses in computer programming to supplement their degree in a particular field, such as accounting, finance, or medicine. This echoes what Rob Short, former corporate vice president for Windows Core Technology at Microsoft, advises: "I recommend strongly that people study an area that really interests them...and then learn computer science to create applications to improve on their area. For example, huge leaps are being made in medicine that are not possible without people who have studied both medicine and computer science." One manager at Microsoft was actually a zoology major.

Companies who use computers for scientific or engineering applications usually prefer college graduates who have a degree in computer or information science, mathematics, engineering, or the physical sciences. Companies who use computers for business applications prefer to hire people who have had college courses in management information systems and business, and who possess strong programming skills. A graduate degree in a related field is required for some jobs.

Most systems programmers hold a four-year degree in computer science. Extensive knowledge of a variety of operating systems is essential for such people. This includes being able to configure an operating system to work with different types of hardware and being able to adapt the operating system to best meet the needs of a particular organization. Systems programmers also must be able to work with database systems, such as DB2, Oracle, or Sybase—and to keep up with these systems as they change.

Although knowledge of traditional programming languages still is important, software programmers are discovering an emphasis on newer, object-oriented languages and tools, such as C++ and Java. In addition, programmers who take the time to become familiar with fourth- and fifth-generation languages that involve graphic user interface and systems programming may see more opportunities for advancement (see the Everyone Knows sidebar in chapter 2 for more information on the generations of computer languages). The motivated person interested in pursuing a career in computers and programming might consider going to a two-year community college or technical school for specialized training. Without a degree, substantial specialized experience or expertise may be needed.

Certification demonstrates a specific level of competence and may provide a competitive advantage. Voluntary certification almost always makes a favorable impression. In addition to language-specific certificates, product vendors or software firms offer certification and may require people who work with their products to be certified. In fact, industry certification is one way to build credibility, which can then open doors to more opportunities.

Helpful Personality Traits

Given the nature of the job, the best programmers are people who can think logically and pay close attention to detail. Programming calls for patience, persistence, and the ability to perform exacting analytical work, especially under pressure. Ingenuity and creativity are particularly important when programmers design solutions and test their work for potential failures. The ability to work with abstract concepts is helpful as well.

Because programmers are expected to work in teams and interact directly with users, general communication and business skills are important, especially for those wanting to advance to managerial positions.

Systems Analysts

Most computer systems analysts have at least a bachelor's degree. For more technically complex jobs, graduate degrees are preferred. However, the level and type of education required will reflect changes in technology. In most cases, the people capable of implementing the newest technologies are the ones who will be in the most demand.

As with computer programmers, for jobs in a technical or scientific environment, it's best to have at least a bachelor's degree in a technical field, such as computer science, information science, applied mathematics, engineering, or the physical sciences. For jobs in a business environment, a bachelor's degree in a business-related field is desirable. Recently, there is a trend whereby employers are seeking individuals who have a master's degree in business administration with a concentration in information systems. In general, employers are looking for people with expertise relevant to a given job.

As has been pointed out, however, people who have degrees in other majors (like zoology!) may find employment as systems analysts if they also have technical skills. Courses in computer science or related subjects combined with practical experience can help people further advance their careers.

Helpful Personality Traits

As with computer programming, people who succeed in this field often possesses strong problem-solving and analytical skills, and the ability to think logically. Because several tasks are often dealt with simultaneously, the ability to concentrate and pay close attention to detail is important. Although these people sometimes work independently, they frequently work in teams on large projects. Therefore, they must have good interpersonal skills and be able to communicate effectively with computer personnel, users, and other staff who may have no technical background.

1Most software engineers have at least a bachelor's degree (the usual college major for applications software engineers is computer science or software engineering) and experience with a variety of computer systems and technologies. Graduate degrees are preferred for some of the more complex jobs. In 2006, about 80 percent of workers had a bachelor's degree or higher.

As with any other field in the computer industry, the successful software engineer is always learning about new technologies and acquiring the skills to master them. In this industry, advancement is often commensurate with experience. Software engineers with advanced degrees in areas such as mathematics and systems design are expected to be particularly in demand by software developers, government agencies, and consulting firms.

Systems software vendors offer certification and training programs, but most training authorities say that program certification alone is not sufficient for the majority of software engineering jobs. However, for software engineers, the Cisco Certified Network Associate (CCNA) certification is absolutely a must. It validates a person's ability to install, configure, operate, and troubleshoot local area network (LAN), wide area network (WAN), and dial-up access services in medium to large networks (500 nodes or more), including use of certain protocols. For server engineers, Microsoft Certified Systems Engineer (MCSE) certification is essential, verifying a person's ability to analyze the operation requirements of any organization and to design and implement business solutions based on either a Windows platform or Windows Server products. For database engineers, it's the Microsoft Certified Database Administrator (MCDBA). People with this credential have proven knowledge in implementing and administering Microsoft SQL Server databases.

When first entering this career, it is not uncommon for a new software engineer to start by testing designs. As experience grows, a person may move to designing and testing software under the guidance of a more senior engineer. Eventually, they may advance to become a project manager, manager of information systems, or chief information officer, especially if they have business skills and training. Some computer software engineers with several years of experience or expertise find opportunities working as systems designers or independent consultants.

Helpful Personality Traits

As with the other computer-related jobs discussed thus far, successful software engineers must have strong problem-solving and analytical skills. They also must be able to communicate effectively with team members, other staff, and the customers they meet. Because they often deal with a number of tasks simultaneously, they must be able to concentrate and pay close attention to detail.

Again, the pattern that emerges as careers in this field are studied is one of always remaining on the cutting edge, looking to areas of advancement and developing one's skills accordingly. To help keep up with changing technology, people often find it beneficial to take continuing education and professional development seminars. These may be offered by employers, software vendors, colleges and universities, private training institutions, and professional computing societies. As with the other positions, software engineers also need skills related to the specific industry in which they work. Engineers working for a bank, for example, should have some expertise in finance so that they understand banks' computer needs.

Database Administrators

This is one area where a formal degree is not quite as important and experience can carry more weight; however, people with a formal education may find their careers advancing further and faster than someone without a formal education. That being said, in some cases, a two-year degree is sufficient, especially if the experience is there. Preferred areas of study include computer science, information science, or management information systems (MIS). MIS programs usually are part of the business school or college, and differ considerably from computer science programs, emphasizing business and management-oriented coursework and business computing courses.

Database administrators can often enhance their opportunities for career advancement by earning certifications. Many employers—and database administrators themselves—regard these certifications as the industry standard. For example, one method of acquiring enough knowledge to get a job as a database administrator is to become certified in database management with a certain software package. Voluntary certification also is available through various organizations associated with computer specialists.

Database administrators may advance into managerial positions, such as chief technology officer, based on their experience managing data and enforcing security

Helpful Personality Traits

People with strong problem-solving and analytical skills, as well as good interpersonal skills, will do well as a database administrator. Because they often deal with a number of tasks simultaneously, the ability to concentrate and pay close attention to detail also is important. Although database administrators sometimes work independently, they frequently work in teams on large projects. As a result, they must be able to communicate effectively with computer personnel, such as programmers and managers, as well as with users or other staff who may have no technical computer background.

As always, technological advances come so rapidly in the computer field that continuous study is necessary to keep one's skills up-to-date. The lazy, unmotivated database administrator is not one that will survive.

Keeping
in Touch

Sort of like a Friendster or MySpace for the business world, LinkedIn (http://www.linkedin.com) "is an interconnected network of experienced professionals from around the world, representing 170 industries and 200 countries. You can find, be introduced to, and collaborate with qualified professionals that you need to work with to accomplish your goals." According to their site, LinkedIn has over 35 million members in over 200 countries and territories around the world; a new member joins LinkedIn approximately every second, and about half of the members are outside the United States; and executives from all Fortune 500 companies are LinkedIn members. Overall, the site has immense value as a networking tool. One member notes, "You have to spend some time and effort to build your network and search to find the right people. But the great thing is that those efforts are multiplied over and over by the slick LinkedIn system."

Because technology is so closely connected to the functioning of businesses, many network/systems administrators come from elsewhere in the business or industry. This background can be useful, in that it helps them to better understand how their networking tools are being used within the organization.

Web Site Designers

Perhaps more than any other computer-related field, Web designers are truly a jack-of-all-trades. This is one of the few computer-related fields where focusing on a specific niche—finance or medicine, for example—may actually limit a person's career options rather than enhance them. There is the "computer-related hat": Web designers need to understand various computer languages, such as HTML, DHTML, ASP, and Java. They need to be familiar with text editors, HTML authoring tools, and graphics and animations tools. Then there is the "writer hat": The truly proficient Web designer also possesses some skill as a writer, often researching, writing, and editing site content so that is easy to read and compelling. Obviously, there's the "art hat": Web designers use images, graphics, and various page elements in such as way as to make a site interesting visually, yet easy to use. The Web abounds with example of both bad and good sites.

In addition, the successful, effective Web designer possess excellent management skills. They are able to focus on the minutiae of a Web site, but can step back and see the bigger picture. A Web site is often the first impression a person has of a company—whether they are researching a potential employer, looking to buy shoes online, or conducting research for a project. To that end, Web designers also ensure that their site can be accessed by a variety of different browsers, that content is kept up-to-date and timely, and that search engine optimization (SEO) techniques are employed so that the site is ranked high by search engines. Consistent branding guidelines may be adhered to so that a person's experience on a site, for example, is similar to the feeling of being in the actual store. Web designers ensure that links work and are current; they may also keep track of traffic statistics. And, as with any computer-related position, the successful Web designer is always assessing new standards, technologies, trends, and products for use with new and existing Web sites.

There are no specific education or training requirements to be a Web designer. Qualifications can vary, depending on the size and

Professional Ethics

Be honest and realistic when it comes to your capabilities and project goals. One of the most common problems is to get halfway into a project and realize there is no way you can complete it in the timeframe required. Perhaps the complexity was underestimated or unanticipated changes are required that affect other parts of the project and now that affects your ability to meet the deadline.

Rather than just working harder and hoping the project will be completed by some miracle, stop and think about the goals of the project. Why are they not being met? Brainstorm ideas and which features can be left out or different ways to tackle the problem. Then get together with everyone involved with the project and explain in detail the problem and your possible solutions. The important thing is to make sure a different approach is truly being taken to solve the problem. As Einstein said, "The definition of insanity is doing the same thing over and over again and expecting a different result."

type of organization and the sophistication of that organization's Web "presence." For example, Amazon may have certain requirements for their Web designers that a smaller company, like a regional chain of hardware stores, does not. Oftentimes, associate's degrees, certificate programs, or relevant experience may be all the qualifications a person needs, although it is important to be aware that some jobs do require applicants to have a bachelor's degree. Concentrations in information technology or other technology-related subjects, graphics design, or combinations of technology and graphics or artistic design may be preferred.

The Web designer who is looking to stay a Web designer may be able to increase his or her demand by finding a niche and developing a client base in that particular field—for example, medical information Web sites. As with any other job in this field, it is important to stay on top of trends and developments. For example, the Web designer who has a solid grasp of search engine optimization (SEO) techniques—writing Web copy so that it is ranked high by major search engines—will be in greater demand than a designer who, while perhaps a talented graphic artist, does not understand these concepts as well. The best-designed site will mean nothing if no one sees it.

The successful Web designer will also have a firm, working understanding of various Internet technologies, such as HTML, Java, and, Perl; security technologies; FTP; electronic mail, and more. Often, knowledge of these languages can help a person to make the jump from Web design to computer programming, for example, or even to project management.

Helpful Personality Traits

Given the wide range of tasks a Web designer may be responsible for, a wide range of skills is often called for. For example, good listening skills are important to ensure that the site's goals and requirements are clearly understood. Effective communication skills are important—as with any computer-related position. Time management skills are needed, as is a strong sense of organization and prioritization. Of course, art or graphic design skills are essential, as is attention to detail.

Computer Support Specialist

A college degree is required for some computer support specialist positions, but certification and relevant experience may be sufficient for others. In any case, strong analytical, problem-solving, and communication skills are essential. Because technical issues often have to be explained to nontechnical users, a computer support specialist who possesses these skills is often even more valuable.

The amount of formal college education a computer support specialist has can vary. A bachelor's degree in computer science or information systems is a prerequisite for some jobs; other jobs may require only a computer-related associate degree. Some companies are becoming more flexible about requiring a college degree for support positions. In the absence of a degree, however, certification and practical experience are essential. Certification training programs, offered by a variety of vendors and product makers, may help some people to qualify for entry-level positions.

Support specialists may advance into positions in which they use what they have learned from customers to improve the design and efficiency of future products. Job promotions usually depend more on performance than on formal education. Eventually, some computer support specialists become software engineers, designing products rather than assisting users. Computer support specialists in hardware and software companies often enjoy great upward mobility; advancement sometimes comes within months of becoming employed.

As technology continues to improve, computer support specialists must strive to acquire new skills and stay on top of technological trends—that is the mantra of the computing industry. Employers, hardware and software vendors, colleges and universities, and private training institutions often provide many continuing education programs. Professional development seminars offered by computing services firms also can enhance skills and advancement opportunities.

Helpful Personality Traits

As mentioned, people interested in becoming a computer support specialist must have strong problem-solving, analytical, and communication skills because troubleshooting and helping others are vital parts of the job. The constant interaction with other computer personnel, customers, and employees requires computer support specialists and systems administrators to communicate effectively on paper, via e-mail, over the phone, or in person. Strong writing skills are useful in preparing manuals for employees and customers.

When Considering a Move

It's not likely that the position a person starts out with in this field is the one he or she remains in throughout their career. Interests change, career paths open up, or the entry-level job is merely a stepping stone to a larger career goal. When looking to make a career move—whether vertically or laterally—consider the following.

Identify Your Key Skills

Your "key skills" include the ones that are actually related to the job you are seeking. For example, knowledge of Java, Perl, and C# computer languages; experience with database administration; or a stint as a computer support specialist provide practical skills relevant to a career in computers and programming. Key skills are often in line with the path on which you plan to take your career.

Fast Facts

According to Neil McAlister of the Web site InfoWorld, in 1978 Gary Theurk, a marketer for Digital Equipment Corporation, stumbled upon a wonderful use for ARPANET. (ARPANET had been developed by the U.S. Department of Defense to allow computer researchers, vendors, and other government contractors to communicate across long distances—in other words, using e-mail.) Instead of addressing an e-mail to one or two people, Gary thought, why not include all of them at once? As the story goes, Gary wanted to announce an open house his company was hosting at which they planned to unveil a new line of mainframes.

The resulting mass-mailing was the world's first spam, and while ARPANET authorities claimed that "appropriate action [would be] taken to preclude its occurrence again," clearly spammers found a way. Spam can range from annoying to entertaining to potentially harmful—so do yourself and your coworkers a favor and just hit the Delete button when it arrives in your inbox. The best way to prevent spam is to stop it in its tracks.

Then there are the skills that make you a good worker. Regardless of the field, there are certain skills that most employers look for in an applicant, such as promptness, reliability, diligence, and work ethic. These are the skills that do not have anything to do with the specific job—or with any job, for that matter—but make a person well suited for a particular career. For example, many jobs in the computers and programming field are ideal for people who are detail-oriented, creative, can think logically, and enjoy solving problems.

Finally, there are transferrable skills—these skills may not have anything to do with computers and programming, per se, but they can certainly help you in that line of work. For example, a person who has experience in bookkeeping might do well as a database administrator. A person who has experience in retail sales might find those skills transfer well to a computer support position. A person who has excellent math skills may find software programming enables him or her to utilize those skills on another level.

Define Your Ideal Job

Your ideal job is more than just a title. When clarifying this in your mind, consider things like the skills you feel you are strongest in and that you want to utilize (or perhaps skills you don't yet possess but want to become proficient in—by developing those skills you can further advance your career!). Consider the work environment you would find ideal: working at home, working for a small company, working for a large company, working a traditional 40-hour-a-week job, working whatever hours a job requires, or perhaps being on call. The environment also extends to the people. Those who want to be surrounded by people who are more creative might be better suited working for a gaming or CGI company. Those who are passionate about giving back to the community may find themselves drawn to a nonprofit that specializes in providing computers for libraries and schools. Location is another factor to consider. Do you want to work in a particular city, such as Seattle, San Diego, or Singapore? Have you had enough of winters in Minnesota and decided that life in Florida is better suited for you? And then there's income. Some people want to make $100,000 a year; for others, $40,000 is sufficient. Keep in mind that you may have to start with the $40,000 salary to get to the $100,000 one.

Be proactive when it comes to your career. Don't just wing it and hope for the best. If you want to succeed, you must have a plan. If you don't have one, find a mentor—whether a manager, another co-worker, or a supervisor—and ask them for advice. However, before latching onto one, you need to think about this person's skills and way of working, and be sure that you do indeed desire to be more like him or her. Keep in mind that if you work with a mentor, others will associate you with this person. That can be a great thing, but it can backfire on you, too. For example, if the person you are considering as a mentor is considered brilliant, but difficult to work with, you may acquire the same reputation.

Things That Can Make or Break Your Interview

Books and Web sites abound with information on the do's and don'ts of interviewing, and while most of that information will not be repeated here, a few points do bear repeating, with an emphasis on how they can help advance a career in computing. What you wear really does matter. Even if the corporate culture at the company is casual and laid back with regard to work attire, that does not mean you should dress that way for your interview. You don't necessarily need to wear a business suit, but your clothes should be clean and wrinkle-free, with no rips or tears. Wear slacks rather than jeans.

Make eye contact when you first meet the person who greets you for your interview, once or twice again while walking to the interview location, and again when you first sit down to do the interview. Shake the person's hand firmly. Act professional and confident.

Along with thoroughly understanding everything you can about the position you are applying for, know how to position your current skills against the job you are after. For example, if your experience up to this point as a network analyst involved supporting 50 computers, you might be feeling confident and worldly—until you find out that the job you are interviewing for requires that you work with customers with 20,000 computers.

Establishing a Professional Reputation

Regardless of how casual your work environment is or how small the company may be, there is no excuse for not acting professionally. If you do not take your career seriously, no one else will. There are things that can firmly establish you as a professional, and there are things that can quickly ruin your reputation.

From a technology standpoint, you can establish yourself as a professional by staying up-to-date on what is happening in the industry. Stay abreast of technological innovations and progress, as well as the processes and tools available. Use the simplest solution possible to meet a project's requirements.

From a computing standpoint, it is important to recognize your limits. One of the easiest ways to ruin your reputation is to get in over your head on something and destroy a customer's computing environment. Computer management tools exist that could allow a person to do this without even realizing it.

Another of the quickest ways you can ruin your professional reputation is by using negative comments. Avoid words like *don't, won't,* and *can't.* For example, rather than saying "I don't work well with negative people," say, "I find working with negative people an enjoyable challenge, although it can be tough and I'd like to avoid it if possible." The first statement implies that you are not adaptable and are unable to work with a variety of people. The latter statement shows that you are flexible and willing to tackle difficult situations.

Everyone
Knows

ROM vs. RAM. People often use the term "memory" when discussing their computer's hard drive. However, this is actually an inaccurate (albeit common) use of the term.

RAM (random access memory) is where programs that are currently being used by the processor are held. This "cache" is cleared when you shut down the computer.

ROM (read only memory) is where all programs on your computer are stored until you need them. This is the hard drive; items stored here stay here until you remove them.

David Patterson, author of *Computer Organization and Design*, uses a great analogy to explain how this works: Think of the hard drive (ROM) as a file cabinet. It contains all of the programs your computer needs to operate. RAM can be thought of as a desktop (an actual desktop, not the virtual "desktop" on your computer!). When you open a program you want to work on, it's like taking a file from the file cabinet and moving it to your desktop. When you are done working on the program, you put the file back into the file cabinet for long-term storage. By that analogy, if you have a system crash or a power failure while working on something on the desktop, it's as if a window opens and a strong breeze blows everything off the desk before you can put it away.

Another reputation-killer is to have people think you are unreliable or picky about the type of work you are willing to do. Again, this goes back to *don't* versus *didn't*. For example, rather than saying that you "don't" do project management, say you "didn't" do project management in your last job but would be willing to try it with guidance where needed.

Be a person who does things and gets things done. Be proactive— look for what needs to be done and be prepared to do whatever it takes to help. Work that you are responsible for should be the highest quality and should be completed on time. Rob Short adds this: "Every project worth doing has problems. Be honest about the problems and about sharing the credit with people who help."

Honesty and accountability also go a long way in establishing a professional reputation. If you didn't do a good job on something, be honest about it. Trying to blame someone else for problems you encountered or as an excuse for the state of your work, or just producing work of low quality when you (and perhaps your boss) knows you are capable of more, will be noticed and remembered. Just as attention to detail is a key skill for many positions in the computing industry, so is it a factor when it comes to one's professional reputation.

Getting Ahead

When asked what strengths or talents make someone well suited for the computer industry, Bill Weiss, worldwide technical community director for Microsoft Services, said, "I think to be successful in this industry, you have to be somewhat of a workaholic. It is definitely not an 8 to 5 kind of industry. Things are constantly changing, and it takes nights and time on weekends to keep up. If someone were attracted to [this industry] purely based on salary opportunities and thought they could [just] get in their eight hours . . . they would not last long. The people who have longevity in this business share a passion, and it enables them to work the longer days because they just like what they do."

Passion is a key theme among the people interviewed for this book. They repeatedly emphasized that the people who did best in this field were passionate about technology and evidence of this passion is what they look for in interview candidates. In fact, candidates that otherwise looked good on paper have lost jobs for the simple reason that the interviewer felt they were not passionate enough about technology. So find an area or application in the computer industry you are passionate about, and the rest will follow.

Beyond that, people who see success in this field can learn and work with little supervision, possess good communication skills (both in speaking and writing), are analytical thinkers, can think outside the box, and can adapt to the ever-changing trends in this industry. Good customer service skills may also be important.

Rob Short has this to add: "People need to learn to be self-critical and take the time to think about how they are doing, relative to their ability and what they want to do, as well as relative to their peers. If people want to run a division or a company, they should think about the experiences that are needed before they can do that.

"In technology, people with the curiosity and drive to learn new things grow faster than others. I tell new people to look at a large system and try to figure out how it *all* goes together. For example, in terms of operating systems, think of typing a key. What happens from the time that key is pressed and picked up by the keyboard driver to the time that character is drawn on the screen? Look at a Web site—ask what happens when someone accesses the page: What scripts run on the client? On the server, exactly what pieces of code run? What data is accessed?

"People who succeed are not afraid to learn from watching what others do. Some people never get beyond looking at the details and have problems with larger projects. The best people can see the large problem abstractly, but understand the details of the pieces and how they fit into the overall picture."

Defining a Career Path

Sometimes, a person enters this field with a specific career path in mind; for others, the path evolves as the career evolves. Both approaches are fine—the key is to be flexible but deliberate. Rob Short, had no formal plan when he started his career. However, "over time," he says, "I realized that I needed to think about the skills [necessary] to survive and advance. One of the most valuable things I've done is earning a master's in computer science while working full-time. ...If I had the opportunity to start again, I'd do more 'foundation' courses early on." For example, a deeper understanding of math and physics may give someone an edge if they want to move into design and development.

In general, the basic career path that people in this field follow is to start with a degree from a technical college or a bachelor's degree in computer science and then to follow that with industry certification, depending on your area of specific interest. The importance of a bachelor's or/and master's degree has been emphasized in this book, although that degree is not necessarily a key to advancement for every position in this field.

The sections that follow explain specific certifications for certain positions in this industry and how they can advance your career.

Certifications

Microsoft Certifications "not only recognize and validate your real-world skills, but they also provide you access to unique resources and offer a life-long career path for developing your IT skills."

INTERVIEW

Recognizing Microsoft Style

Roberta Croly

Operations manager for Microsoft Services' chief technology officer

What's the first thing you notice about a potential candidate when meeting them?

The clothes they wear because it's the first thing I see. Can't help but notice them. I don't think an interviewee needs to deck out in a swanky business suit, but clean clothes, no tears, rips, no jeans, not crumpled, not rumpled. When I see jeans and a t-shirt on the street, I think casual, easy-going. Because my mind set changes to business mode when I walk through the doors of my building, when I see an interviewee in jeans and a t-shirt (and I have seen it, more than once), I immediately think Rebel Without a Cause and we may have problems. I see khakis and a collared shirt, and I think Bill Gates and we mean business.

What are the top mistakes you've seen interview candidates make?

Number one, not looking at me. I once had an interview with a person who wouldn't look at me. Nothing exudes lack of confidence more than no eye contact. Make eye contact when you first meet, once or twice while walking to the interview location, and definitely when you first sit down to the do the interview. After that, as needed.

The second, not asking me questions. Clarifying questions, questions about the business, the job, the company. Yes, you are being interviewed, but I also think the interviewee is interviewing the company. Read up on the company, the business, the business group. See if you can find out about the team members and managers. Investigate.

Certifications are available for nearly every Microsoft application or technology and are useful for a wide range of computer careers, including IT professionals, developers, office workers, home users, and technology trainers.

In case you are thinking that certification won't help you advance your career, consider this. According to a survey conducted by Microsoft, 66 percent of managers believe that certifications improve the level of service offered to end users and consumers, and 75 percent believe that certifications are important to team performance.

Then write down five questions and take a writing implement to write at least one question per interview. Do ask the questions, and do ask all interviewers the same five questions. You can make some good fit determinations based on how all interviewers answer the same question. Also, with experience you ask better questions. I once had an interviewer ask me if I had any questions, and I said no. She asked if I had questions about team organization and future plans. I said no. Those were the two questions that kept me from getting the job.

What sets one candidate apart from another aside from experience? If you have two equally qualified candidates but can only choose one, how do you choose?
Confidence! From my first impressions of the person sitting in the lobby (or pacing nervously) to their mannerisms as we walk to my office to their preparedness (or not) during the interview. Cold interviews (no prep time taken) are good for seeing what's available, but if you really want to land the job, be prepared.

According to author and career coach Mike Farr, while it's impossible to be prepared to answer every single question an employer may ask you, if you are prepared to answer the tough ones that invariably come up, you should be able to handle most any question the interviewer throws your way. These questions are:

Why should I hire you?
Why don't you tell me about yourself?
What are your major strengths?
What are your major weaknesses?
What sort of pay do you expect to receive?
How does your previous experience relate to the jobs we have here?
What are your plans for the future?
What will your former employer (or references) say about you?
Why are you looking for this type of position, and why here?
Why don't you tell me about your personal situation?

So what certifications does Microsoft offer? Five different levels are available:

Desktop Support Series
Technology Series
Professional Series
Master Series
Architect Series

The Desktop Support series validates desktop computer skills for the 2007 Microsoft Office System and other versions of Microsoft Office, along with the Windows Vista operating system. Certifications in this series demonstrate advanced, cross-industry and cross-job capabilities, such as managing budgets and presentations, and supporting organizations. Two certifications are available: Microsoft Certified Application Specialist (MCAS) and Microsoft Office Specialist (MOS).

The Technology Series is designed to validate a person's ability to implement, build, troubleshoot, and debug a particular Microsoft technology, such as Windows Server, Microsoft .NET Framework, or Microsoft SQL Server. In order to earn a particular certification, a person must pass anywhere from one to three exams and have at least one year of relevant experience. A person who earns a certification is considered a Microsoft Certified Technology Specialist (MCTS) and more than 30 certifications are currently available.

The Professional Series certification validates a comprehensive set of job-related skills, such as project management, system design, operations management, and planning. Employers often consider such a certification a reliable indicator of on-the-job-performance. In order to earn this certification, a person must pass anywhere from one to three exams and have one or more technology (MCTS) certifications. Two certifications are available, based on job roles: Microsoft Certified IT Professional and Microsoft Certified Professional Developer.

A Master Series certifications demonstrates that a person can successfully design and implement solutions that solve highly complex business challenges. The certifications focus on specific technologies, such as Microsoft Exchange Server 2007, Windows Server 2008–Directory, and Microsoft Office SharePoint Server 2007. The courses provide expert-level classroom training and labs that incorporate real-world customer scenarios and include both computer- and lab-based exams. The instructors are Microsoft experts and Microsoft global network partners who are experts in their disciplines.

The Architect Series also provides classroom training and labs based on real-world scenarios and a person who earns certification as a Microsoft Certified Architect (MCA) is considered an industry expert in IT architecture. To obtain this certification, applicants must definitively demonstrate seven competencies of business acumen and technological proficiency during a Review Board interview with a panel of industry experts. Two different certification tracks are available: MCA Technology and MCA Infrastructure.

For database administrators, certification in two languages in particular can give someone an edge in advancing their career: SQL and Oracle. Various organizations and schools offer such tests. Typically, such tests demonstrate a person's proficiency in implementing and maintaining databases using specific instructions and specifications. A thorough knowledge of the product (SQL or Oracle) is demonstrated, along with an understanding of how to use available tools and how to explore the user interface.

These are not the only languages in which certification is available. Nearly every language or profession mentioned in this book offers certification at differing levels. Chapter 6 provides information to get you started.

Certifications are available for Web designers as well, starting with basic certification and getting progressively more complex. CIW, the Certified Internet Web Professional program, offers an Associate certification, referred to as the Foundations exam. It demonstrates a person's proficiency with Internet technology, page authoring, and networking basics.

Another basic certification is the Certified Web Designer (CWD) certification. This was offered by the Association of Web Professionals (AWP). However, that organization is no longer in existence. Fortunately, Jupiter Systems purchased the contents and intellectual property rights to this exam and has continued the certification tests. The exam, which is online, demonstrates proficiency in basic Internet technology and Web design skills. Web Manager and Technician Certifications are also available.

WebYoda's Online Webmaster (WOW) Academy is "committed to offering the best Webmaster training courses, assessment exams, and certification options to meet the needs of aspiring Web professionals." To that end, they offer a CAW (Certified Associate Webmaster) certification. Successful completion of certification demonstrates basic proficiency in the following areas:

Internet Basics
Markup and Scripting
Web Graphics
Web Multimedia
Web Site Design
Web Site Management
Legal Issues
Web Accessibility

Web Project Management
Web Business Management
Web Marketing

The World Wide Web Consortium (WC3) is the group that sets the standards for the Internet. They offer a basic, 70-question exam that results in an HTML Developer Certificate and tests applicants on HTML, XHTML, and Cascading Style Sheet (CSS).

Brainbench offers several certification preparation exams. Several of the skills-related exams can be combined to earn the Brainbench Certified Internet Professional (BCIP) certification.

From there, intermediate-level Web design certifications are available to the aspiring Web developer. Knowledge of coding and scripting, along with relevant job experience is necessary in order to earn the certifications discussed next. The Associate Webmaster Professional (AWP) exam is also offered by WebYoda. Topics cover Internet fundamentals, basic and advanced HTML and XHTML knowledge, and expertise with CSS.

Those who have more experience with programming languages and one year of working with ColdFusion, may wish to pursue this exam. ColdFusion is an application server and software language used for Internet application development, such as for dynamic Web sites.

Web designers who are proficient in Dreamweaver who also have experience with coding, graphics, and Web site management may want to consider earning a Dreamweaver MX Certification. Dreamweaver is a Web development application that hides the HTML code details of pages from users, which makes it an ideal application for people who do not have a lot of coding experience to create web pages and sites. The Dreamweaver MX Certification, however, demonstrates a thorough understanding of the Dreamweaver application, Web page design, Web page authoring, and supporting technologies.

Adobe Flash (previously called Macromedia Flash) is a multimedia platform created by Macromedia and currently developed and distributed by Adobe Systems. It is commonly used to create animation, advertisements, and various Web page components; to integrate video into Web pages; and more recently, to develop rich Internet applications.

Macromedia offers two tracks for the Flash certification: Flash MX Designer and Flash MX Developer. The Designer exam requires knowledge of Flash motion design, optimization, and publishing. The

Developer exam requires knowledge of relational database design, along with one to two years of experience in software development and Web design.

Advanced Web design certifications will require a mastery of skills and technologies that go well beyond Internet and design concepts. Depending on the certification path a person chooses, testing may demonstrate skills and knowledge in e-business concepts, marketing, security, management, and more advanced scripting skills.

The CIW program offers several different tracks for its CIW Master Certification, including Administrator, Developer, Web Site Manager, and Security Analyst. Each track requires multiple exams on a variety of subjects.

The CWP certification, offered by the IAW, requires that a person obtain the AWP certification first. Completion of this certification demonstrates proficiency in Web design and graphics, e-business concepts, intermediate Java skills, and e-marketing concepts.

When considering a career in the computer and programming industry and what path that career will follow, it should be clear that there is a great deal of overlap in many areas. For the most part, the bottom rung of the ladder is an entry-level position, with advancement occurring as experience and perhaps degrees and/or certification is attained. At some point, people with years of experience in a given field may decide to go into teaching, helping to launch the next generation of programmers, developers, and so on. Where this career goes depends largely on your interests and your passions. Furthermore, just because a career starts in one area, this doesn't mean it must stay on that path. For example, a person who starts out as a database analyst may become a systems analyst, a networking consultant, a Web designer, a data miner, or a professor of computer science. Someone whose career path starts in programming may move into a specific area of science, medicine, or engineering; this person may become a statistician, a bioinformation specialist, a quality assurance specialist, a systems or database analyst, a data miner, a technical writer/editor, a systems consultant, or a user interface designer.

The thing to keep in mind when plotting a career path is to remain flexible. Technology changes at a speed and in ways that cannot always be imagined. For long-term success, you have to adapt on the fly as technology changes.

Trends that, as of this writing, are emerging in this field and that may shape the path a person's career takes include things like a shift from centralized to decentralized computing, "cloud" computing (Internet-based development and use of computer technology), virtualization, and "green" IT.

Success in this field requires three things: a passion for technology, an ability to pay attention to detail, and the tenacity and innate ability to learn and understand its complexity. Build a foundation of as much math, physics, and computer science as you can, find a niche that interests you, and see where it takes you. The bottom line is that in order to advance this career, it is important to stay current with technology, take classes and workshops, and read trade journals. Respect and learn from those who have been in the business for a long time, even though they may not be "techie."

Effective Business Communication Techniques

One of the most important skills a person in this field can have is the ability to talk "techie" to non-techies—this was emphasized repeatedly by those interviewed for this book. One of the most frustrating things for an office worker, for example, who is having a computer problem and needs help solving it is to have the computer support specialist talk over their heads. Learn how to explain technologies concepts in a way that isn't demeaning to the non-technical person, yet assures understanding—and don't talk down to them. Make sure the non-techies are satisfied with the explanation and all questions have been answered.

This is also important when in meetings or similar situations where, for example, a database administrator is explaining how a system will scale up and require more resources sooner rather than later. Avoid slipping into overuse of jargon and acronyms. Just because you are familiar with these terms does not mean everyone else around you is. Also, this concept is important to keep in mind no matter what form your communication is in—whether face-to-face, on the phone, via e-mail or instant messaging, or a business proposal, keep your audience and their level of understanding about what it is you do in mind.

Managing Your Time Effectively

While sometimes a person can get in over their head because they overestimate their skills, in many cases, this occurs because of improper time management. Developing techniques and strategies that help you manage your time effectively will, in turn, reduce your stress level and increase productivity. This advice holds true for anyone, in any position, but people in the computing field—perhaps programmers and analysts in particular—are especially prone to falling into this trap.

When you have projects with hard and fast deadlines, prioritize your schedule accordingly. Block out this time in your schedule if you need to, and let coworkers and others know that you need to be undisturbed for a given amount of time—even if it is just an hour. That hour of concentrated work could be worth four hours of work with interruptions. If you need to (and if this is possible, given your work environment), consider working in a separate room.

Some people are at their sharpest in the morning; others are more effective in the afternoon. Know what your "best" time of the day is and tackle your most challenging tasks then. If you still find it hard to stay on task, try to figure out where the block lies. Are you lacking information to complete the tasks? Are you lacking motivation? Are you unclear about the goals? Positively identifying some of these problem areas will often lead to solutions, which, in turn, leads to better time management.

If you find yourself chronically behind in tasks and routinely missing deadlines, for the sake of your professional reputation, consider keeping a "time diary." Just as people who are struggling with their weight or their finances keep a log for a week or a month, noting where every penny goes or what they put in their mouth, so, too, can keeping a log of where and how you are spending your time show you where simple changes can help improve efficiency. For example, a 2007 survey conducted on behalf of Fuser.com) found that 87 percent of U.S. Internet users spend at least seven hours a week managing their e-mail—that's practically an entire workday!

One well-known, effective time management technique is the basic "to do" list. Every evening, before you leave work, make a list of what you need to accomplish the next day. Prioritize it in terms of urgency and importance. Aim to achieve as much as possible, but always remain flexible so that you can take on unexpected tasks if necessary.

While it's natural to want to say "yes" to everything that is asked of you, if you try and juggle too many balls in the air at once, you're bound to drop a few—and your professional reputation can suffer. If you are asked to take on a task and you know that you will not be able to meet the deadline, you must communicate that up front.

Be honest—don't give a vague answer like "I'm not sure." Consider negotiating on the timing. For example, say, "I can't do it today, but I would be happy to do it by the end of the week." If this task is one you simply cannot turn down, work with your supervisor or other colleagues, explain the situation to them, and come up with a plan so that other deadlines are not missed. Learning to say no is not easy, but you will earn more respect by understanding and respecting your own limits—and communicating them clearly and effectively—rather than saying "yes" to everything and paying the price down the road.

Chapter 5

Talk Like a Pro

The following in-depth glossary explains industry jargon, key terminology, phrases, concepts, and general business language that will help you hit the ground running before you even start launching your new career in computers and technology. For more information on these terms, see either the *Microsoft Press Computer Dictionary, Third Edition*, or Chapter 6.

abacus A manual counting device that predates computers and calculators consisting of a frame holding parallel rods with moveable "counters" on them.

Advanced Research Projects Agency (ARPA) Eventually renamed DARPA (Defense Advanced Research Projects Agency), this program was established in 1958 to protect the United States against "technological surprises," such as when the Soviet Union launched *Sputnik* into space in 1957, beating the United States in the "space race." This agency is responsible for the development of new technology for use by the military, and has been responsible for funding the development of many technologies, including computer networking.

algorithm A procedure or formula for solving a problem. In most cases, an algorithm must end after the problem is solved. The word comes from the name of the mathematician, Mohammed ibn-Musa al-Khwarizmi, who was part of the royal court in Baghdad and lived from about 780–850.

analog As the word pertains to computing, it refers to a computer that uses continuous electrical, mechanical, or hydraulic quantities to model the problem being solved. With an analog computer, numbers are represented by directly measurable quantities, such as voltages or rotations.

API (application programming interface) A set of routines used by a program to direct the performance of procedures by an operating system. APIs can be language-independent (utilizing the particular syntax and elements of a programming language) or language-independent (written so that they can be called from several programming languages).

array A data structure consisting of a group of elements that are accessed by indexing. In most programming languages, each element has the same data type and the array occupies a contiguous area of storage.

artificial intelligence Also known simply as "AI," this field of computer science has to do with the intelligence of machines. John McCarthy, an American computer scientist, coined the term in 1956 as "the science and engineering of making intelligent machines."

Fast Facts

The first computer bug really *was* a bug! As legend has it, in 1945, while working on a prototype of the Mark II, Grace Murray Hopper discovered a moth that had caused a relay failure. The moth was taped into the logbook alongside the official report, which stated: "First actual case of a bug being found." Use of the word *bug* to describe a glitch, however, actually goes back to about 1878.

BIOS (basic input/output system) The first code run by a computer when it is turned on. The BIOS is responsible for identifying, testing, and initializing system devices such as the video display card, hard disk, and floppy disk and other hardware. Then, the computer is brought to what is called a "known state" so that software stored on compatible media can be loaded, executed, and given control of the PC.

binary Essentially, the term refers to something with two components, alternatives, or outcomes. In terms of computer science, the word is often used in reference to the binary number system in which values are expressed in terms of two digits: 1 and 0.

bit   A piece of data represented by either a zero or a one.

blog   A contraction of the term "Web log," this is an online journal or diary. Many are maintained by an individual, and typically provide commentary on news, current events, or a particular topic.

broadband   A type of communications system in which the medium used for transmission carries multiple messages simultaneously. This form of communication is typically for wide area networks.

bug   An error in computer coding or logic that causes a program to function incorrectly or to produce incorrect or unexpected results.

byte   A byte is comprised of eight bits. These groups of 8 bits can represent up to 256 different values and can correspond to a variety of different symbols, letters or instructions.

bytecode   The term refers to various forms of instruction sets designed for efficient execution by a software interpreter, as well as being suitable for further compilation into machine code. Different parts may often be stored in separate files, similar to object modules, but dynamically loaded during execution.

cache   A temporary storage area where frequently accessed data can be stored for rapid access. Once data is stored in the cache, it can be accessed from here rather than being retrieved or calculated again. This cuts down on access time.

capacitor   An electronic component that typically consists of two conductive plates separated by an insulating, nonconductive material.

Cascading Style Sheet (CSS)   A computer language used to describe the presentation of a document written in a markup language—most commonly HTML and XHTML, but it can be applied to any kind of XML document. Cascading Style Sheets include information on how the Web page should appear, including colors, fonts, layout, and other aspects of document presentation.

central processing unit (CPU)   A single chip, such as a microprocessor, or a series of chips that performs arithmetic and logical calculations, and that times and controls the operations of the other elements of the system.

clock rate   Often incorrectly referred to as clock speed, this is the rate at which the clock in a device, such as a computer, oscillates. The clock rate is usually given in terms of hertz (Hz—a hertz is one cycle per second).

cloud computing A style of computing in which typically real-time scalable resources are provided "as a service over the Internet to users who need not have knowledge of, expertise in, or control over the technology infrastructure that supports them," according to authors Galen Gruman and Eric Knorr. The term "cloud" is a metaphor for the Internet, based on how it is depicted in computer network diagrams, and is an abstraction for the complex infrastructure it conceals.

CLR (Common Language Runtime) Microsoft's implementation of the Common Language Infrastructure (CLI) standard, which defines an execution environment for program code. The CLR runs a form of bytecode called the Common Intermediate Language (CIL). Developers using the CLR write code in a language such as C# or VB.Net. At compile time, a .NET compiler converts such code into CIL code. At runtime, the CLR's compiler converts the CIL code into native code of the operating system.

compiler A computer program that transforms source code written in one computer language (called the source language) into another computer language (called the target language).

concern A particular set of behaviors needed by a computer program. A concern can be as general as database interaction or as specific as performing a calculation.

conductor A substance that transmits electricity.

cookie A simple piece of data that a Web server stores on a client system. It is used to identify users, to instruct the server to send a customized version of a particular Web page, to submit account information, and so on.

cross-cutting concern Aspects of a program that affect other concerns. These concerns often cannot be easily broken down from the rest of the system in either design or implementation, and result in scattering or tangling of the program or both.

data mining The process of identifying commercially useful patterns or relationships in large amounts of data. While the term has acquired a somewhat negative connotation in recent years, at its heart, it is simply the process of turning raw data into useful information. It's what enables sites like Netflix to recommend other movies you might enjoy based on your (and others') recent picks.

desktop Characteristic of programs such as Microsoft Windows and Apple Macintosh, this term refers to the on-screen work area that uses icons, menus in such a way that it simulates how a person uses a physical desktop to manage tasks and workflow.

digital   This term refers to a computer system that uses discontinuous values, usually but not always symbolized numerically, to represent information for input, processing, transmission, storage, etc. By contrast, analog systems use a continuous range of values to represent information. Although digital representations are discrete, the information represented can be either discrete (numbers, letters, or icons) or continuous (sounds or images).

document object model   A platform- and language-independent standard object model for representing HTML or XML documents as well as an application programming interface (API) for querying, traversing, and manipulating such documents.

driver   A hardware device or program that controls or regulates another device. The term is commonly used in conjunction with devices such as printers or disk drives. A print driver, for example, enables a computer and printer to communicate and work together.

Electronic Numerical Integrator And Computer (ENIAC)   Conceived and designed by John Mauchly and Presper Eckert, this behemoth of a machine was designed and built to calculate artillery firing tables for the U.S. Army's Ballistic Research Laboratory and could solve a wide range of computing problems.

e-mail   Short for electronic mail, at its heart, this is an electronic text message, but can include the transmission of files, applications, graphics, and more.

Ethernet   A standard by which local area networks are connected by coaxial cable, fiber-optic cable, or twisted-pair wiring in a bus or star topology.

extranet   An extension of a company's intranet using World Wide Web technology. An extranet is often used to allow a company's customers, suppliers, and others to gain limited access to the company's intranet for specific purposes.

fault tolerance   The ability of a computer or operating system to respond to a catastrophic event or fault, such as a power outage or hardware failure in a way that ensures no data is lost and any work in progress is not corrupted.

fiber optics   A technology that uses light beams to transmit information along optical fibers. Light has a higher frequency than other types of radiation, such as radio waves, and a single fiber-optic channel can carry more information that most other forms of transmission. As of this writing, some companies are starting to offer Internet and television service over fiber-optic lines.

File Transfer Protocol (FTP) The protocol used for copying files to and from remote computer systems on a network.

firmware Permanent commands, data, or programs that the computer needs to function correctly.

FORTRAN Short for FORmula TRANslation, this compiled, structured language is considered the first high-level computer language. It gave rise to such concepts as variables, expressions, and statements. Originally developed by IBM in the 1950s for scientific and engineering applications, FORTRAN is now used in computationally intensive areas such as numerical weather prediction, finite element analysis, computational fluid dynamics, computational physics, and computational chemistry.

function Also known as a subroutine, this is the purpose of or action carried out by a program or routine.

functional programming A style of programming in which the evaluation of expressions is emphasized rather than the carrying out of commands. Examples include C, C++, Python, and Java.

graphical user interface A type of operating environment that represents programs, files, and options through the use of menus, icons, and dialog boxes. A user selects and activates these items by pointing and clicking with a mouse or using a keyboard.

"green" computing The study and practice of using computing resources efficiently. The goals are to reduce the use of hazardous materials, maximize energy efficiency during the product's lifetime, and promote recyclability or biodegradability of defunct products and factory waste.

hack   While the term often has nefarious connotations, it simply refers to creatively altering the behavior or an application or operating system by modifying its code rather than running the program and using it in the traditional manner.

hardware   The physical components of a computer system, such as printers, mice, keyboards, and the case.

Horn clause   A clause with, at most, one positive literal (in mathematical terms, a literal is an atomic formula). See Chapter 6 for a reference to an in-depth article on such clauses.

hypertext   Coined in 1965 by Ted Nelson, an American sociologist, philosopher, and pioneer of information technology, the term refers to text with references (called hyperlinks) to other text that the reader can immediately follow, usually by a mouse click. The World Wide Web is the largest example of hypertext.

Hypertext Markup Language (HTML)   The standard language used for Web pages. Special identifiers, called tags, are used to indicate paragraph breaks, line spacing, font type, font size, graphics, and more. HTML indicates to the Web browser how a Web page should be displayed.

Hypertext Transfer Protocol (HTTP)   The client/server protocol used to access information on the World Wide Web.

identifier   Any text string used as a label, such as the name of a procedure or a variable in a program.

index (v)   To create and use a list or table that contains reference information pointing to stored data; to locate information stored in a table by adding an offset amount, called the index, to the base address of the table.

Information Technology Infrastructure Library (ITIL)   A registered trademark of the United Kingdom's Office of Government Commerce, this is a set of concepts and policies for managing IT infrastructure, development and operations. It provides detailed descriptions of several important IT practices, with comprehensive checklists, tasks, and procedures that can be tailored to any organization.

instance   In object-oriented programming, this is an object in relation to the class in which it belongs. An instance may contain data or instructions.

integrated circuit   Also known as a microchip, this is a miniature electronic circuit that contains several connected elements, such as transistors (these assist the flow of electricity) and resistors (these resist the flow of electricity).

intranet   A network designed for use within a company or organization. It often uses applications associated with the Internet, such as Web pages, FTP sites, and e-mail, but is accessible only to those within the company or organization.

IP telephony   Also called Voice over Internet Protocol (VoIP), this term refers to a family of transmission technologies for the delivery of voice communications over IP networks such as the Internet or other packet-switched networks.

kernel   The core of an operating system. It manages memory, files, and peripheral devices; maintains the time and date; launches applications; and allocates system resources.

kilobyte   A unit of data consisting of 1,024 bytes. Often abbreviated as K, KB, or Kbyte.

language   A specific pattern of binary digital information.

laptop   A small, portable computer that, these days, is nearly as powerful as its desktop brethren. Most can run the same software as a desktop computer and can use similar peripheral devices, such as mice, sound cards, and external drives.

lazy evaluation   A programming mechanism that allows an evaluation action to be performed only when needed and only to a certain extent. It is designed to allow a program to handle large data objects in a timely, effective manner.

linear equation   An algebraic equation in which each term is either a constant or the product of a constant and the first power of a single variable. Linear equations can, however, have more than one variable.

log   A record of transactions or activities that take place on a computer system.

logarithm   The exponent that indicates the power to which a base number is raised to produce a given number. For example, the logarithm of 1,000 to the base 10 is 3, because you must multiply 10 by 3 to get 1,000; thus 10 x 10 x 10 = 1000. Computer languages such as C and BASIC include functions for calculating natural algorithms.

logic programming   A type of programming in which a program consists of facts and relationships, from which the language is expected to draw conclusions based on these facts.

loop   A set of statements in a program that is executed repeatedly either a fixed number of times or until a condition is true or false.

macro   A set of keystrokes and related instructions that are recorded and saved under a short key code or macro name. When the set of keystrokes is typed or pressed, the instructions are carried out.

magnetic core memory   An early form of random access computer memory that used small magnetic ceramic rings—cores—through which wires were threaded to store information. Although computer memory long ago moved to silicon chips, memory is still occasionally called "core."

mainframe   Also called a "supercomputer," this is a high-level computer designed for intensive computing tasks. A mainframe computer is often shared by multiple users, who connect to it through terminals.

malware   An umbrella term combining the words malicious and software, and used to refer to a variety of forms of hostile, intrusive, or annoying software or program code, such as worms, viruses, Trojan horses, and more.

megaflops Also known as MFLOPS, this is an acronym for "million floating-point operations per second" and is a measure of computing speed.

memory   A device where information can be stored and retrieved. This may be a tape drive or a disk drive (external devices), or the RAM that is connected directly to the computer.

method   In object-oriented programming, this is a process performed by an object when it receives a message.

middleware   Computer software that connects other software components or applications. It includes Web servers, application servers, and similar tools that support application development and delivery.

Moore's law   Named after Intel co-found Gordon E. Moore, this refers to a trend Moore observed whereby the number of transistors that can be placed inexpensively on an integrated circuit has increased exponentially, doubling approximately every two years. Moore's law has become something of a benchmark in the computing industry—the more it gained acceptance, the more it became a tangible goal. However, in an interview on April 13, 2005, Moore stated that the law cannot be sustained indefinitely. He said, "It can't continue forever. The nature of exponentials is that you push them out and eventually disaster happens." At this point, quantum computers may take over.

motherboard   The main circuit board of a computer, containing the primary components of the system: the processor, main memory, bus controller, connector, and support circuitry.

multimedia   The combination of sound, graphics, and video. This can also refer to a subset of hypermedia, which combines these elements with hypertext.

multiprocessing   The use of two or more central processing units within a single computer system. Also, to the ability of a system to support more than one processor and/or the ability to allocate tasks between them. The objective in any case is increased speed and computing power.

multitasking   The ability of a computer system to work on more than one task at a time.

natural language   Any language that is spoken, signed, or written by humans for general-purpose communication. Compare to computer language, which is a machine-readable artificial language designed to express computations that can be performed by a machine, namely, a computer.

.NET Framework   A software framework that is available with several Microsoft Windows operating systems. It includes a large library of coded solutions to prevent common programming problems and a virtual machine that manages the execution of programs written specifically for the framework. This is a key Microsoft offering and is intended to be used by most new applications created for the Windows platform.

netbook   A small, portable computer that relies on wireless communication for access to the Internet. Netbooks are designed primarily for sending and receiving e-mail and browsing the Web. With not much more in the way of capabilities, it can be thought of as a slimmed-down laptop.

network   A group of computers and associated devices that are connected either permanently (through cables, for example) or temporarily (such as through a telephone connection). Networks can range in size from just a few users to a large geographic area.

neural network   With regard to computer science (bioinformatics, in particular), this term refers to a network of interconnected programming constructs that imitate the properties of biological neurons (called artificial neurons). These are often used to gain an understanding of biological neural networks or to solve artificial intelligence problems.

On the Cutting Edge

When a person is suffering from a heart attack, seconds count and life-and-death decisions often have to be made in a split second. A new type of computer software is helping doctors make the decisions faster and more accurately. An international group of researchers, led by the University of Edinburgh, has developed a program that helps doctors identify patients at high risk of heart attack in no time. Key facts—such as a patient's age, medical history, and blood pressure—as well as information derived from immediate blood samples and kidney tests, are input into the program and then matched with data derived from thousands of other coronary cases. Using the outcomes of these previous cases as a guide, the software will not only give an accurate assessment of the current patient's conditions, but also recommend possible treatment. More importantly, it will be able to predict the likelihood of the patient suffering a heart attack, and even their chances of dying in the coming months.

node As it relates to networking, a node is a device that facilitates communication with other network devices. A router or even a computer can act as a node. As it relates to data structures, a node is a location that stores data and links to one or more nodes below it—think of it as a building block of sorts.

object-oriented programming In terms of software, a program is viewed as a collection of discrete objects that are themselves collections of self-contained collections of data structures that interact with other objects.

open-source (adj) In reference to computer programming, this term refers to the free exchange and collaboration of developers and producers. The definition put forth by Bruce Perens, a well-known computer programmer, is widely recognized as the "real" definition: "A broad, general type of software license that makes source code available to the general public with relaxed or nonexistent copyright restrictions."

operator A symbol or other character indicating an operation that acts on one or more elements.

operator overloading The assignment of more than one function to a particular operator, with the implication that the operation performed will vary, depending on the data type involved.

packet A unit of information that is transmitted in its entirety from one device to another on a network.

packet switching A message-delivery technique in which small units of information (packets) are relayed through stations in a computer network along the best route available between the source and the destination. The Internet is an example of a packet-switching network.

peripheral device An ancillary device connected to a computer and controlled by it. Examples include (but are not limited to) speakers, joysticks, keyboards, mice, modems, and printers.

phishing This is an e-mail attempt by someone to gain personal information for nefarious uses. Phishing e-mails may appear to be from a legitimate source, such as a bank, and often trick the recipient to verify personal information, like an account number or Social Security number, by claiming that an account is in danger of being closed, for example. The recipient, believing the e-mail is genuine, provides the desired information, opening him- or herself up to potential identity theft.

podcast A series of digital media files, usually audio or video, that is made available for download via Web syndication. The syndication aspect is what separates podcasts from other files accessible by direct download or streaming.

processor Also called the central processing unit (CPU), this is the device that interprets and carries out instructions—in other words, it is the "brain" of the computer.

program A sequence of instructions that tells the hardware of a computer what operations to perform on data.

"pull" technology A form of Internet-based communication in which data or a program is retrieved from a server to a client at the client's request. For example, using a Web browser to request a particular Web site is a form of pull technology.

"push" technology A form of Internet-based communication in which data or a program is sent from a server to a client at the server's request. Instant messaging and e-mail are forms of push technology.

recursivity Also called recursion, this is a method of defining functions in which the function being defined is applied within its own definition. The term is also used more generally to describe a process of repeating objects in a self-similar way. Used improperly, recursivity can cause a program—or even an entire system—to crash.

register (n)   A set of bits of high-speed memory within a microprocessor used to hold data for a particular purpose.

relational database   A database that stores information in tables and conducts searches by using data in a specified column (or columns) to find additional data in another table. The rows in a table represent records, and the columns represent fields.

relay (n)   A switch activated by an electrical signal. Its use allows another signal to be activated without the need for human intervention.

résumé   A document outlining a person's job history, duties, responsibilities, publications, and other achievements.

routine   Any section of code that can be executed within a program.

search engine optimization (SEO)   An Internet marketing strategy that considers how users search and what they search for. For example, a Web site administrator and designer might look to improve the volume and quality of traffic to her company's Web site from search engines by including phrases in the text on Web pages that the target audience will use.

Silicon Valley   A term referring to the region of Santa Clara Valley south of Stanford University. Its introduction is attributed to journalist Don Hoeffler, who used it in a series of articles in 1971.

software   These are the computer programs or instructions that make hardware work. In general, software can be thought of as one of two types. System software refers to a computer's operating system. Applications perform the tasks for which people use computers—for example, word processing programs, spreadsheet programs, and databases.

Software as a Service (SaaS)   A means of providing applications to customers on demand. With this type of technology, software vendors may make the application available for download on their Web site, or the application may be sent to a user's computer, laptop, cellular phone, or other device.

spyware   Computer software that is installed surreptitiously on a personal computer to intercept or take partial control over the user's interaction with the computer, without his or her specific consent. Spyware programs can collect various types of personal information, such as Internet surfing habits and sites that have been visited, and can also interfere with user control of the computer in other ways, such as installing additional software and redirecting Web browser activity.

subroutine   Another word for routine; however, it usually refers to sections of code that are short and called on a more frequent basis.

switch (n)   A circuit element that has two states: on and off.

system   At its most basic level, any grouping of components that work together to perform a task are functioning as a system. A hardware system, for example, consists of the microprocessor, computer chips, circuitry, peripheral devices, and input and output devices. An operating system consists of program files, data files, and other applications used to process information.

telecommunications   The transmission and reception of data, television, sounds, faxes—any form of information—through the use of electrical or fiber-optic signals sent over wires or fibers, respectively, or through the air.

TeleType machine   An essentially obsolete electromechanical typewriter that was used to communicate typed messages from one point to another point (or several points at once) over a variety of communications channels—from wires, to radio wave, to microwaves. A form of this device is still in use by the deaf for typed communications over the telephone.

Telnet   A protocol that allows an Internet user to log on to and enter commands on a remote computer linked to the Internet.

time sharing   The use of a computer system by more than one user at the same time. This is achieved through multitasking—computing resources are shared so that the computer can work on more than one task at a time.

transistor   A solid-state circuit component with at least three terminals in which a voltage or current controls the flow of another current. A transistor is commonly used to amplify a signal, and is the fundamental building block of computers, radios, phones, and other electronic devices.

Transmission Control Protocol/Internet Protocol (TCP/IP)   A protocol developed by the Department of Defense for communication between computers. It is the de facto standard for data transmission over networks, including the Internet.

Trojan horse   A destructive program disguised as a game, utility, or application that seems harmless. When run, a Trojan horse does something harmful to the computer system while appearing to do something useful. The name comes from the ploy the Greeks used to finally enter the city of Troy during the Trojan War. After a fruitless 10-year siege, the Greeks built a huge figure of a horse, in which a group of men hid. The Greeks pretended to sail away, and the Trojans pulled the horse into their city as a victory trophy. At night, the Greek force crept out of the Horse and opened the gates for the rest of the Greek army, which had sailed back under cover of night. The Greek army entered and destroyed the city, decisively ending the war.

UNIX   A powerful, multiuser, multitasking operating system widely used in servers and workstations. It was originally developed by Ken Thompson and Dennis Ritchie at AT&T Bell Laboratories in 1969 for use on microcomputers.

videocast   Short for "video podcast" and sometimes shortened to vidcast or vodcast, this refers to the online delivery of video on demand, similar to a podcast.

virus   An often-malicious program that infects a computer system by inserting copies of itself into certain files. A true computer virus can only spread from one computer to another (in some form of executable code) when its host is taken to the target computer; for instance because a user sent it over a network or the Internet, or carried it on a removable medium such as a floppy disk, CD, or USB drive.

Web browser   An application that uses HTML to enable a user to browse the World Wide Web (although they can also be used to display content on internal networks and private file systems). With a browser, a user can view and interact with text, images, videos, music, games, and other information typically on a Web site.

Webinar   A conference in which live meetings or presentations can be conducted over the Internet.

wide area network (WAN)   A communications network that connects geographically separated areas.

Wi-Fi   Contrary to popular belief, this is not an acronym—or even a combination of two separate words. Rather, this is a registered trademark of the Wi-Fi Alliance (a global, nonprofit organization devoted to promoting the growth of wireless local area networks, or WLANs). A Wi-Fi device meets certain standards that promote interoperability among wireless devices, ranging from personal computers, laptops, and peripherals to smartphones.

World Wide Web Consortium (WC3)   The mission of World Wide Web Consortium is "to lead the World Wide Web to its full potential by developing protocols and guidelines that ensure long-term growth for the Web." The organization does this by publishing open (non-proprietary) standards for Web languages and protocols.

worm   A program that propagates itself across computers, typically by creating copies of itself in each computer's memory. Unlike viruses, a worm does not need human help to spread to other computers.

Chapter 6

Resources

This book was designed to be as comprehensive a guide as possible for those launching a career in the field of computers and programming. However, some areas are beyond the scope of this book. As a result, the following sections provide sources of more information, ranging from books and periodicals to Web sites, schools, training programs, and more. The Web site addresses provided were current as of the writing of this book.

Associations and Organizations

It can be hard—if not impossible—to advance a career in computers and programming without joining a professional association. As with many fields, networking—that is, who you know and who knows you—is critical. Not all jobs are posted publicly, and the right word in someone's ear could land you that key position you have been working so hard to achieve. Again, coworkers or mentors can advise you (and perhaps even sponsor you, if need be) as to what organizations and associations are of the most benefit.

The Alliance of Technology and Women is a nonprofit organization that "supports women and men worldwide who share the common interests of empowering women in technology, increasing the number of women in executive roles, and encouraging women and girls to enter technology fields." (http://www.atwinternational.org)

American Society for Information Science and Technology is aimed at information professionals "leading the search for new and better theories, techniques, and technologies to improve access to information." The group's more than 4,000 members work in a variety of industries, ranging from computer science, linguistics, management, librarianship, engineering, law, medicine, chemistry, and education. (http://asis.org/about.html)

Association for Computing and Machinery touts itself as "the premier membership organization for computing professionals, delivering resources that advance computing as a science and a profession; enable professional development; and promote policies and research that benefit society." People looking to launch a career in this field may find the Career & Job Center particularly useful. (http://www.acm.org)

Association for Multimedia Communications "promotes understanding of technology, e-learning, and e-business." Part of the organization's mission is to help member achieve success in their chosen field. They do this by offering education and networking opportunities. Members also can search for job opportunities. (http://www.amcomm.org)

Association for the Advancement of Artificial Intelligence is a nonprofit scientific society devoted to "advancing the scientific understanding of the mechanisms underlying thought and intelligent behavior and their embodiment in machines. AAAI also aims to increase public understanding of artificial intelligence, improve the teaching and training of AI practitioners, and provide guidance for research planners and funders concerning the importance and potential of current AI developments and future directions." (http://www.aaai.org/home.html)

Association for Women in Computing is a national, nonprofit, professional organization designed to "promote awareness on issues affecting women in the computing industry, further the professional development and advancement of women in computing, and encourage women to enter computing as a career." Information on scholarships, a job network, and regular community events are also included. The link cited here is for the Puget Sound chapter, but chapters are available throughout the United States. (http://www.awcps.org)

Association of Information Technology Professionals offers "opportunities for IT leadership and education through partnerships with industry, government and academia." With more than

Everyone
Knows

Requests for Comments (RFC) are documents published by the Internet Engineering Task Force (IETF) describing methods, behaviors, research, or innovations applicable to the working of the Internet and Internet-connected systems. While the acronym is certainly not unique to the computer industry, this is its most well-known context. It is a mistake to think of them as standards. Not all RFCs achieve such a lofty rank. RFCs are assigned one of the following categories: S for Standard (fully adopted), D for Draft (initial testing phase), P for Proposed (entry-level phase), H for Historic (this RFC is considered obsolete). The RFC Editor assigns each RFC a unique serial number. Once assigned a number and published, an RFC is never rescinded or modified; if the document requires amendments, the authors publish a revised document. Together, the RFCs compose a continuous, historical record of the evolution of Internet standards and practices.

7,000 members, the organization provides education, information on relevant IT issues, and networking forums.   (http://aitp.org)

CERT part of the Software Engineering Institute, was set up after the Morris worm incident (see the sidebar) to "coordinate communication among experts during security emergencies and to help prevent future incidents." Areas of focus include software assurance, making systems more secure, organizational security, coordinating responses to threats, and providing education and training.   (http://www.cert.org)

Computer Security Institute is the first and leading educational membership organization for information security professionals. "At the forefront of security trends and research, CSI provides a forum for security professionals to learn, share, even debate the latest thinking on security strategies and technologies." CSI holds two conferences annually: CSI SX in spring, in conjunction with Interop, and the Annual Computer Security Conference and Exhibition in the fall. These conferences are designed for those entering the field, as well as experienced practitioners.   (http://www.gocsi.com)

HDI, originally known as the Help Desk Institute, is the "largest association for IT service and support professionals" with more than 7,500 members. As such, the organization "produces numerous publications, hosts several symposiums and two conferences each year, and certifies hundreds of help desk and service desk professionals each month." (http://www.thinkhdi.com)

IEEE Computer Society is the world's leading organization of computing professionals, with more than 85,000 members. Founded in 1946, and the largest of the 39 societies of the Institute of Electrical and Electronics Engineers (IEEE), the Computer Society is "dedicated to advancing the theory and application of computer and information-processing technology." The organization offers technical journals, magazines, conferences, books, conference publications, and online courses. Those who are switching from a different career to one in computers and programming should consider the IEEE CS Certified Software Development Professional (CSDP) program; recent graduates looking to launch a career in this field should consider the Certified Software Development Associate (CSDA) credential. (http://www.computer .org/portal/site/ieeecs/index.jsp)

Information Technology Association of America was created to "represent and enhance the competitive interests of the U.S. information technology and electronics industries ... by providing leadership in business development, public policy advocacy, market forecasting and standards development to more than 350 corporate members." Members range from small start-ups to industry leaders offering services, system integration, Internet, telecommunications, software, electronics and hardware solutions to the public and commercial sector markets. (http://www.itaa.org)

Institute for Certification of Computing Professionals has dedicated itself to the "establishment of high professional standards for the computer industry." To that end, the group promotes these standards by offering certification in two major professional designations: Certified Computing Professional (CCP) and Associate Computing Professional (ACP). (http://iccp.org)

Internet Society is a nonprofit organization designed to "provide leadership in Internet-related standards, education, and policy." The group is dedicated to "ensuring the open development, evolution, and use of the Internet for the benefit of people throughout the world." In addition, the Internet Society is the home base for the Internet Engineering Task Force (IETF) and the Internet Architecture Board (IAB). (http://www.isoc.org/isoc)

Open Group "is a vendor-neutral and technology-neutral consortium, whose vision of 'Boundaryless Information Flow' will enable access to integrated information, within and among enterprises, based on open standards and global interoperability." (http://www.opengroup.org)

Society for Information Management is "a community of thought leaders who share experiences and rich intellectual capital, and who explore future IT direction." The group offers meetings and networking opportunities, publications, and training tools in the form of Webinars, Webcasts, an online library, and best practices documents. (http://simnet.org)

Society of Internet Professionals is a nonprofit group designed to represent the interests of Internet professionals. The group's mission is "to enhance educational and professional standards for Internet professionals." As such, SIP has created the Accredited Internet Professional (AIP) designation. (http://www.sipgroup.org)

Society of Women Engineers supports the "goals of stimulating women to achieve full potential in careers as engineers and leaders, expanding the image of the engineering profession as a positive force in improving the quality of life, and demonstrating the value of diversity." (http://societyofwomenengineers.swe.org)

Best Practice

To turn on or to turn off...that is the question. And the answer may spark more debate than it seems to warrant. Some people fervently recommend leaving a computer on as long as possible, believing that a computer's components come under the most stress when turned off and on, and so a failure is less likely if the computer is left alone. However, while true in theory (or if computer were turned on and off 50 times an hour, every hour), in reality, today's PCs are built better than this. For those who are still not convinced, the power management features that are standard on all PCs enable users to put the machine in "sleep mode" when not in use and "wake" it up in a matter of seconds.

Software Engineering Institute is federally funded research and development center that has "served as a national resource in software engineering, computer security, and process improvement." The organization is part of Carnegie Mellon University and works closely with defense and government organizations, industry, and academia. (http://www.sei.cmu.edu)

Software & Information Industry Association is the "principal trade association for the software and digital content industry. SIIA provides global services in government relations, business development, corporate education, and intellectual property protection to the leading companies that are setting the pace for the digital age." (http://www.siia.net/default.asp)

World Wide Web Consortium, which was created by Tim Berners-Lee, was created to "lead the World Wide Web to its full potential by developing protocols and guidelines that ensure long-term growth for the Web." The organization pursues this mission through the creation of Web standards and guidelines. (http://www.w3.org)

Books and Periodicals

The list of items provided here is by no means exhaustive. Rather, it is designed to provide a jumping-off point, and one book or periodical may take two readers in two different directions. Check out your favorite online bookstore and see what recommendations others have.

It should come as no surprise that there are fewer hard-copy magazines and journals these days—most are available online. However, even the print versions have a Web site, with access to archived issues, reviews, discussion groups—even job boards, in some cases. Some periodicals are aimed at a specific niche-for example, network administration—and others are more general in scope. Anyone looking to advance their career would be wise to subscribe to these or other periodicals and read them faithfully. Coworkers can also provide reading suggestions.

Books

A History of the Personal Computer: The People and the Technology. By Roy A. Allan (Allan Publishing, date unknown). This online book provides a detailed look at the development of the personal computers, from the early 1960s through the 1990s.

Also included is information on noteworthy names in the field,
a brief look at the history of computer peripherals (keyboards
and mice, for example), and corporate activities.   (http://www
.retrocomputing.net/info/allan/)

How the Web Was Won: Microsoft from Windows to the Web. By Paul
Andrews (Broadway Books, 1999). While it might seem that
Microsoft has also been a powerhouse of computing, this was not
always the case. In 1993, when the Internet came to the forefront
of popular culture, things looked bad for Windows. The Internet
ran on Unix; the World Wide Web, not Windows, was connecting
the world; and a new software program called Mosaic made finding and reading Web documents easy. This book describes how
Microsoft clawed its way to the lofty position it holds today—going
from a relatively unknown company to a monopoly-like behemoth—and the handful of Internet devotees who led the way.

***Weaving the Web: The Original Design and Ultimate Destiny of the
World Wide Web.*** By Tim Berners-Lee (HarperCollins, 2000).
This fascinating memoir, written by the man who first conceived of the World Wide Web, details the history and philosophy behind the Internet. Berners-Lee describes how the idea for
the Web came about, how it was developed, and the quantum
leap in programming it launched. The release of graphical browsers such as Netscape Navigator and Internet Explorer made the
Web easier for home users to navigate and led to the explosion of
commercialization opportunities—the dot-com era. Berners-Lee
also explains why he does not think using the Internet to make
money is a bad thing, discusses issues surrounding privacy and
pornography, and offers his prediction for the future of the Web.

Secrets of the Rock Star Programmers: Riding the IT Crest. By Ed
Burn (McGraw-Hill Osborne Media, 2008). Get inside the minds
of such programming legends as Adrian Colyer, a pioneer of
aspect-oriented programming tools; Chris Wilson, lead architect of Microsoft Internet Explorer; James Gosling, the "father of
Java"; Dave Thomas, a pioneer of object-oriented software; and
Max Levchin, co-founder and former CTO of PayPal. Learn how
to take your programming skills—and your career—to the next
level by designing programs that rock.

Occupational Outlook Handbook. By Bureau of Labor Statistics, U.S.
Department of Labor (2008–09 Edition, Computer Support Specialists and Systems Administrators). While this online reference
provided most of the material in Chapter 3, readers will find more

Problem
Solving

So despite everyone's best efforts, from time to time it happens: A product is released to customers, who then discover a problem with the item in question. Perhaps a feature doesn't work the way it's supposed to or a driver doesn't install the way it should. When it happens (and it's a common scenario), the only thing to do is determine exactly what the problem is (this often entails using customer feedback), where the root cause lies (this often involves going back and checking computer logs), how to fix it, and then how to get that fix to the customers as quickly as possible. Another important step is to document the problem internally to ensure that it doesn't happen again.

detailed information on the typical working environment for the positions described in this book, related occupations, additional data on projections and outlook, and more.   (http://www.bls .gov/oco/ocos268.htm).

A History of Modern Computing, **2nd ed.** By Paul E. Ceruzzi (The MIT Press, 2003). This book provides a comprehensive account of the history of the digital computer. The author begins with the creation of ENIAC in 1945 and then details the computer's development from the giant, room-size mainframes of the 1950s, the smaller and nimbler minicomputers of the 1960s, the rise of hobbyists and their effect on the history of the PC, up through the design of computer networks that are prevalent today. What makes this book particularly interesting is how Ceruzzi grounds the history of the computer in the context of history at large.

Top 100 Computer and Technical Careers. By Michael Farr (JIST Works, 2007). Chapters 3 and 4 described the most popular career paths many in the computers and programming industry travel. However, there are dozens and dozens of other related jobs. Farr's book describes these various careers, which might include industries readers had not previously considered. The book also offers a job-match grid tool for those still looking to determine a career path, advice on effective job searching, and information on trends in jobs and industries.

Tribes: We Need You to Lead Us. By Seth Godwin (Penguin Group, 2008). While not a book on computers or programming per se, Ramon Infante, Worldwide Community Director for Unified Communications at Microsoft, considered it an invaluable read for anyone looking to launch a career in this field. According to Godin, tribes are groups of people aligned around an idea, connected to a leader and to each other. They make the world work—and always have. The Web has enabled an explosion of all kinds of tribes. They are easier than ever to find, organize, and lead—and yet, not enough people are doing so. Godin believes this is the hottest growth industry today and explains why and how "tribal leaders" can emerge.

Where Wizards Stay Up Late: The Origins of the Internet. By Katie Hafner (Simon and Schuster, 1998). This book provides an in-depth look at the revolutionary science behind the creation of the Internet and the brilliant (albeit at times eccentric) scientists and engineers at universities and agencies worldwide that made it possible, with a focus on how the Cold War era led to its conception.

Electronic Brains: Stories from the Dawn of the Computer Age. By Mike Hally (Joseph Henry Press, 2005). This is a great book for those looking to better understand how social and historical factors in general shaped the history of computing. Rather than focusing on the history of the technology, however, this book concentrates more on the people. In addition, it provides information on Australian, British, American, and Soviet computer pioneers, and touches on social issues like the Cold War and IBM's business relationship with Nazi Germany.

Career Opportunities in Computers and Cyberspace. By Harry Henderson (Ferguson Books, 2004). This book explains both the opportunities and challenges for those launching a career in computers and programming. As with Michael Farr's book, this book describes careers readers can consider beyond the traditional programmer, developer, or database administrator—such as specialized librarians, manufacturing, sales, and more.

The Universal History of Computing: From the Abacus to the Quantum Computer. By Georges Ifrah (John Wiley & Sons, 2001). This book traces the history of computing in depth, beginning with the development of the abacus, then moving to the invention of the binary system three centuries ago and mechanical and electronic computers, and ending with a look at the aspirations to create quantum computers.

The Age of Spiritual Machines: When Computers Exceed Human Intelligence. By Ray Kurzweil (Viking, 1999). According to author Ray Kurzweil, by the year 2020, computers will have outpaced the human brain in terms of intelligence and computational power. An expert on artificial intelligence, Kurzweil postulates his "law of time and chaos" whereby technological evolution moves at an exponential pace, time speeds up as order increases, and vice versa. He believes it is possible, if not inevitable, for computers to become more conscious and that the problems this presents need to be addressed now rather than later.

Go To: The Story of the Math Majors, Bridge Players, Engineers, Chess Wizards, Maverick Scientists, and Iconoclasts—the Programmers Who Created the Software Revolution. By Steve Lohr (Basic Books, 2001). This is the fascinating story of the scientific revolution that made the new economy possible—software—told through the unsung heroes of programming and their achievements. Of course, Apple and Microsoft are covered, but Lohr also explores how FORTRAN and COBOL languages were developed and delves into the open-source world.

Microsoft Press Computer Dictionary, **3rd ed.,** (Microsoft Press, 1997). This dictionary focuses on providing beginning and intermediate computer users with a solid grounding in terms, technologies, and concepts related to productivity software, databases, networks, and communications technologies. Frequent online updates to the Web are also available.

The Hacker Crackdown. By Bruce Sterling (Bantam, 1993). While this book may seem like ancient history, it is far from it. Those looking to learn more about the early days of the Internet and computer programming will find this book a fast-paced, informative read. The book begins with the birth of cyberspace and the first hackers—teenage boys who exploited vulnerabilities in AT&T's switching systems to wreak havoc—and traces the ethical and legal issues that emerged as law enforcement moved online. Sterling introduces some of the early notable hackers, as well as the people at the FBI whose job it was to apprehend them, and shows how three distinct segments of "cyberculture" emerged: the hackers, the cybercops, and the cyber-civil libertarians who were (and are) determined to protect Internet users' privacy at all costs.

The Elements of Style. By William Strunk and E.B. White (Penguin, 2007). This timeless classic is an invaluable reference guide for how to write clearly and succinctly—for those both in and out of the computer field. It explains basic principles of grammar in plain English and—interestingly enough—is the only style guide to have appeared on the best-seller lists.

Beginning Programming for Dummies. By Wally Wang (Wiley Pub., 2004). As part of the popular Dummies series, this book is a great primer for those new to programming. The intent with this book is for people to start writing programs as quickly as possible. Tips are provided on how to choose the best programming language for a particular project. Topics include creating interactive Web sites, programming multiple platform devices, using algorithms, using compilers, and more. Programming for Windows, Linux, Macintosh, Palm PCs, and Pocket PCs is discussed.

Periodicals

Bioinformatics is focused on new developments in genome bioinformatics and computational biology.   http://bioinformatics .oxfordjournals.org)

BusinessWeek may not seem particularly relevant at first glance to someone new to the field of computers. However, with articles on technology, investing, companies, innovation, and more, the astute person may, just by paying a little attention, identify upcoming trends in this industry and take advantage of them. (http://www.businessweek.com)

PC Magazine, which is available in both print and online forms, delivers "authoritative, labs-based comparative reviews of computing and Internet products...placed in the unique context of today's business technology landscape." (http://www.pcmag.com)

Wired magazine, which is available in both print and online forms, reports on how technology affects culture, the economy, and politics. (http://www.wired.com)

Web Sites

Certification/Training

As mentioned in Chapter 4, certifications and degrees are not everything, and they certainly are no substitute for experience—especially since this field changes so rapidly. Yet many people interviewed for this book repeatedly stressed the importance of taking classes on a regular basis and getting certifications. It is one of the primary keys to getting ahead.

Adobe Certified site is designed to provide visitors with "everything they need to know about the certification programs—from taking the tests to promoting their newfound status." Explore the certifications available, find a training center, and prepare for the exam. The Adobe Training page (http://www.adobe.com/training/) feature online resources and events that teach participants the skills they need to further their career through hands-on tasks and real-world scenarios. (http://www.adobe.com/support/training/certified_professional_program)

Brainbench was founded in January 1998 with the mission of "delivering easy-to-use assessment products that predict success on the job." Training and certification products cover a wide range of Internet technologies. Visitors can look for tests based on specific skills, categories, or jobs. (http://www.brainbench.com)

Certified Internet Web Professional Program claims to be "the world's fastest growing vendor-neutral Internet certification for the knowledge economy." The organization offers dual enrollment and college credit opportunities, comprehensive instructor and student resources, and high-quality content that addresses topics such as Web site design, database design, JavaScript, project management, and more. (http://www.ciwcertified.com)

Global Knowledge touts itself as the "worldwide leader in IT and business training." The company delivers training through special centers, private facilities, and the Internet. Their IT and business training courses cover a wide range of areas, from networking and wireless technologies, IP telephony, security, programming, operating systems, and more. (http://www.globalknowledge.com)

International Webmasters Association is a nonprofit professional association with the goal of providing educational and certification standards for Web professionals. With more than 60 online, instructor-led classes and four Web certificates, IWA's accomplishments include "the industry's first guidelines for ethical and professional standards, Web certification and education programs, specialized employment resources, and technical assistance to individuals and businesses." (http://www.iwanet.org)

Microsoft Certifications page provides a detailed overview of the various certifications that are available, what they can do for your career, where to register, study guides, and special offers. (http://www.microsoft.com/learning/mcp/default.mspx)

SkillPath provides training and conferences for a wide range of industries, including business skills, computer skills, and more. Audio conferences and Webinars are available, as are on-site training sessions. (http://www.skillpath.com/index.html/gs/gse001)

W3 Schools offers a wide range of training and certification in areas ranging from HTML, XML, browser and server scripting, Web building, multimedia applications, and more. (http://www. w3schools.com)

WOW Academy is committed to offering the "best Webmaster training courses, assessment exams, and certification options to meet the needs of aspiring Web professionals." (http://wowacademy.com/wowacademy/wowcertifications02.cfm)

U.S. News & World Report 2009 survey According to this survey the best colleges to obtain an undergraduate degree in computer engineering, where the highest degrees offered are a bachelor's or master's are:

Rose-Hulman Institute of Technology (Terre Haute, IN):
http://www .rose-hulman.edu

Cal Poly—San Luis Obispo (San Luis Obispo, CA):
http://www.calpoly.edu

Harvey Mudd College (Claremont, CA):
http://www.hmc.edu

Cooper Union (New York, NY):
http://www.cooper.edu

San Jose State University (San Jose, CA):
http://www.sjsu.edu

Bucknell University (Lewisburg, PA):
http://www.bucknell.edu

Fast Facts

The Morris worm is considered the first worm on the Internet—and it was certainly the first to gain widespread attention. Interestingly enough, it also led to the first conviction in the United States under the Computer Fraud and Abuse Act (designed to address federal computer-related offenses and hacking of computer systems). Its designer, Robert Tappan Morris, a student at Cornell University, was sentenced to three years' probation, 400 hours of community service, and a fine of $10,000.

The best colleges to obtain an undergraduate degree in computer engineering where the highest degree offered is a doctorate include:

Massachusetts Institute of Technology (Cambridge, MA):
http://web.mit.edu/

Stanford University (Stanford, CA):
http://www.stanford.edu

Carnegie Mellon University (Pittsburgh, PA):
http://www.cmu.edu

University of California-Berkeley (Berkeley, CA):
http://www.berkeley.edu

University of Illinois-Urbana-Champaign (Champaign, IL):
http://www.uiuc.edu

Georgia Institute of Technology (Atlanta, GA):
http://www.gatech.edu/welcome

University of Michigan-Ann Arbor (Ann Arbor, MI):
http://www.umich.edu

California Institute of Technology (Pasadena, CA):
http://www.caltech.edu

Cornell University (Ithaca, NY):
http://www.cornell.edu

University of Texas-Austin (Austin, TX):
http://www.utexas.edu

U.S. News & World Report states that rankings of undergraduate programs accredited by the Accreditation Board for Engineering and Technology are "based solely on the judgments of deans and senior faculty, who rated each program they are familiar with on a scale from 1 (marginal) to 5 (distinguished)." There are separate rankings for colleges that offer doctoral degrees and those whose highest degree is a bachelor's or master's because "[r]esearch at the graduate level often influences the undergraduate curriculum, and schools with doctoral programs in engineering tend to have the widest possible range of offerings."

General Information

AllConferences.com This site that provides a comprehensive list of computer-related conferences. Areas of focus include artificial intelligence, databases, mobile computing, open source, security, virtual reality, and more. (http://www.allconferences.com/computers)

Analog Vs. Digital Computing | World of Computer Science Summary See this site for a more in-depth explanation of the differences between analog and digital computing. (http://www.bookrags.com/research/analog-vs-digital-computing-wcs)

Dr. Dobb's Journal offers content covering all languages, platforms, and tools. The site has merged with several magazines, such as *Windows Developer Magazine, Systems Administrators Magazine,* and *Software Developers Magazine.* Articles explore new technologies, programming styles, tricks of the trade, and more. In addition, a Career Center allows visitors to post their resume and browse available jobs. (http://www.ddj.com)

"History of Computer Languages and Their Evolution." This site provides a thorough history of computers languages—from the first languages and their applications, how other languages built upon them, and more. (http://www.scriptol.org/history.php)

IEEE "Timeline of Computing History." This detailed chronology, put together by the Institute of Electrical and Electronics Engineers (IEEE), traces the history of computing—starting with 4000 B.C. and ending with 1996 (it has yet to be updated beyond this year as of this writing). It is a fascinating yet concise snapshot of how the concept of computing came about and where humans took it. http://www.computer.org/portal/cms_docs_ieeecs/ieeecs/about/history/timeline.pdf.

InfoWorld "identifies and promotes emerging technology segments that add unique value for the organizations that implement them, as well as the vendors that provide those solutions." The site includes "hands-on analysis and evaluation, as well as expert commentary on issues surrounding emerging technologies and products." http://www.infoworld.com

Linux Journal considers itself the "most trusted-source of information" for the Linux community. The magazine provides tips and tricks, in-depth tutorials, product reviews, insights from leading Linux personalities, and more. http://www.linuxjournal.com

Network Computing, part of the Information Week Business Technology network, offers a wealth of information on virtualization, security, network management, enterprise applications, and more. (http://www.networkcomputing.com)

Silicon Strategies is a "news and analysis resource for semiconductor professionals ... [giving] industry and investment professionals the most comprehensive coverage of semiconductor manufacturing and industry worldwide." (http://www.eetimes.com/news/semi/index.jhtml;jsessionid=DL13GA1O3XAKEQSNDLRSKH0C JUNN2JVN)

Slashdot is a technology-related news Web site that features user-submitted and editor-evaluated current affairs news with an admittedly "nerdy" slant. (http://slashdot.org)

Snopes.com This well-known site aimed at debunking or verifying various urban legends and myths, has an extensive section on computers. Whether you browse the site for fun, edification, or both, you'll know whether passing on an e-mail about an alleged virus will make you look well informed or like you don't know a modem from a mouse. (http://www.snopes.com/computer /computer.asp#virus)

Index

A

abacus, 109
accountability, honesty and,
   97–98, 108
adding machine, 4
Adobe Flash, certification by,
   104–105
Adobe Systems, 43–44
Advanced Research Projects
   Agency (ARPA), 109
Advanced Research Projects
   Agency Network (ARPANET),
   14–15, 17, 94
AI (artificial intelligence), 36–38,
   110, 126
Aiken, Howard, 6–7, 8, 25
airline incident, computer error
   causing, 2
algorithms, 6, 18, 21, 109
Allan, Roy, 9, 11
analog, 110, 140
analytical engine, 5
Andreesen, Marc, 17
API (application programming
   interface), 110
Apple, Inc., x, 17, 44
application programming interface
   (API), 110
applications programmer/analyst,
   27, 28, 57
Architect Series certification,
   Microsoft, 102
ARPA (Advanced Research
   Projects Agency), 109
ARPANET (Advanced Research
   Projects Agency Network),
   14–15, 17, 94
array, 110
artificial intelligence (AI), 36–38,
   55, 110, 126

Aspect for Java, 23
assembly languages, 18
associations/organizations,
   125–130
Atanasoff, John, 2, 7
Atanasoff Berry Computer (ABC),
   7
authoring, SLATES feature of Web
   2.0, 39
AutoCAD, 42
Autocode (1952), 20

B

Babbage, Charles, 5, 56
Baldwin, Frank, 14
BASIC (Beginner's All-purpose
   Symbolic Instruction Code), 9,
   21
basic input/output system (BIOS),
   110
BBS (bulletin board systems), 17
Beginner's All-purpose Symbolic
   Instruction Code (BASIC), 9, 21
Berners-Lee, Tim, 17, 39, 130
Bina, Eric, 17
binary system, 4, 7, 18, 38–39, 110
BIOS (basic input/output system),
   110
bit, 11, 111
blog, 111
books/periodicals, 130–136
Brainbench, certification by, 104,
   137
broadband, 111
   access, 40–41
browsing, 17–18, 123
bug, 110, 111
bulletin board systems (BBS), 17
business communication,
   techniques for effective, 106–108

business model, Dell's, 13
byte, 111
    first use of term, 11
bytecode, 111

C

cache, 111
CAD (computer-aided design), 73
calculations, 3–4
    binary system of, 4, 7
    history of mechanical devices
        for, 6
calculators, computers v., 25
capacitor, 111
career(s)
    changing jobs to advance in,
        83–84, 93–96
    choosing, 43, 105
    computer industry, range of,
        xv
    satisfaction, 84
    successful, 83–84, 106
career advancement, 98–99
    certification and, 100
    computer programmers, 85
    computer support specialist,
        92–93
    defining career path for,
        99–106
    defining ideal job and, 95
    identifying key skills for, 93–94
    passion and, 98
    software engineer, 87
career path, defining, 99–106
    certification and, 99–106
    industry crossover in, 105
Carissan, E. O., 5
Cascading Style Sheet (CSS), 111
CASE (computer-assisted software
    engineering), 56–57
CCNA (Cisco Certified Network
    Association), 87
CEATEC (Combined Exhibition of
    Advanced Technologies), 51

central processing unit (CPU), 111
CERT, 127
certification, 99–106, 136,
    137–138. *See also* education/skill
    requirements
    computer support specialist, 92
    database administrator, 87, 88
    database engineer, 87
    desktop publisher, 102
    industry crossover and, 102
    language, programming, 103
    media resources for training
        and, 136–139
    Microsoft Corporation
        programs for, 87, 99–103
    server engineer, 87
    software engineer, 87
    systems analysts, 87
    training and, 102
    value of, 99, 100
    Web site designer, 103–105
    WOW, 103–104
Certified Internet Web
    Professional (CIW) program,
    103, 137
certified public accountant (CPA),
    63
Certified Web Designer (CWD),
    103, 105
Ceruzzi, Paul, 7–8
chief technology officer, 62,
    100–101
chips, microprocessor, 9, 10, 14
    invention of, 10
chronology, computer history,
    23–25, 140
Church, Alonzo, 6
Church-Turing thesis, 6
circuits, packets replacing, 15
Cisco Certified Network
    Association (CCNA), 87
CIW (Certified Internet Web Pro-
    fessional) program, 103, 105
clock rate, 111

cloud computing, 37, 38, 106, 112
CLR (Common Language Runtime), 112
ColdFusion, 104
The Combined Exhibition of Advanced Technologies (CEATEC), 51
COmmon Business Oriented Language, 21
Common Language Runtime (CLR), 112
communication. *See also* business communication; telecommunications
   industry jargon/business language terms for, 109–124
   "techie" to non-techies, 106
companies
   big v. small, 49–50
   major computer, 41–50
   R&D of, 43
   statistics on major, 43–48
   up/coming, 48–49
compiler, 112
computer(s)
   "bug," 110
   calculators v., 25
   "computer" term and, 1–2
   debate on turning off/leaving on, 129
   development of modern, 5–8
   early, 4–5
   first large-scale digital, 6–7
   invention of, 2–3
   owners, 6
   personal, 9, 10–13
   second-generation, 8
   security, 3, 64, 70, 127
   speed, 13–14
   third-generation, 9–10
   UNIVAC, 8, 33
computer-aided design (CAD), 73
computer-assisted software engineering (CASE), 56–57

computer engineers, employment/wage statistics for, 31
computer hardware manufacturing technician, 74
computer industry. *See also* key positions; trends, computer industry
   major companies in, 41–50
   range of careers in, xv
   resources/web sites, 140
   sectors, 49
   women in, 52–53, 56, 125, 126, 129
   world market and, 40–41
computer professionals, vii
computer programmers, 56–57
   areas of interest, 84
   career advancement for, 85
   education/skill requirements for, 84–85
   employment/wage statistics on, 26–28
   first, 56
   personality traits helpful to, 85–86
   two types of, 57
computer programming. *See also* languages, computer programming
   functional, 19
   logic, 20, 116
   object-oriented, 19, 27–28, 85, 119
   open-source, 119
computer-related office positions, 80–82
   data entry operator, 81
   desktop publisher, 81, 102
   statistician, 81–82
   systems integrator, 82
computer support specialist
   certification of, 92
   education/skill requirements for, 92–93

employment/wage statistics
　on, 34–35
industry sectors employing,
　34, 35
personality traits helpful to,
　93
computer systems design/related
　service industry, 26–27, 28, 30,
　31, 32, 35
The Computex trade show, 51
computing
　cloud, 37, 38, 106, 112
　digital, 4, 6–7, 113, 140
　quantum, 38–39
　utility, 37
concern, 112
conductor, 112
conferences, 50–52, 140
consulting services, 31, 32
consumer market, computer
　history and, 10–13
"Convergence Age," 40
cookie, 112
corporate culture, viii
CPA (certified public accountant),
　63
Croly, Roberta, on Microsoft style,
　100–101
CWD (Certified Web Designer),
　103

D
data mining, 112
database administrator, 62–63
　certification of, 87, 88
　education/skill requirements
　　for, 32, 88–89
　employment/wage statistics
　　on, 32
　industry sectors employing, 32
　outsourcing not applicable to,
　　52–53
　personality traits helpful to,
　　89–90

database analyst, 57–58
database engineer, certification
　of, 87
databases, 17, 47
declarative languages, 19
Dell, business model of, 12–13
Dell, Inc., statistics on, 44–45
Dell, Michael S., 12–13
Department of Defense, U.S., 94
desktop, 112–113
　computers, 17
desktop publisher, 81
　certification of, 102
Desktop Support certification
　series, 102
digital computing, 113, 140
　basis of, 4
　first large-scale computer for,
　　6–7
document object model, 113
driver, 113

E
earnings. See employment/wage
　statistics
Eckert, Presper, 7–8
education/skill requirements, viii.
　See also certification
　career choices and, 43
　computer programmer, 84–85
　computer support specialist,
　　92–93
　database administrator, 32,
　　88–89
　resources for, 138–139
　software engineers, 87
　systems analyst, 30, 86
　Web site designer, 90–92
Einstein, Albert, 91
Electronic Numerical Integrator
　and Computer (ENIAC), 7–8,
　113
Eleksen Group PLC, 15
e-mail, 94, 107, 113

employment/wage statistics, 26–35
    computer programmers,
        26–28
    industry sectors and, 26–35
    network/systems
        administrators, 32
    software developers, 28
    software engineers, 30–31
    support specialists, 34–35
    systems analysts, 28–30
    Web site designers, 33–34
EnergyStar program, EPA's, 38
ENIAC (Electronic Numerical
    Integrator and Computer), 7–8,
    33, 113
ENQUIRE database, 17
Environmental Protection Agency
    (EPA), 38
errors, computer, 2, 3
Ethernet, 15, 113
ethics, professional, 91
expert systems, AI and, 36
extensions, SLATES feature of
    Web 2.0, 39
extranet, 113
eye tracking, 42

F
fault tolerance, 113
fiber optics, 113–114
fifth-generation computers, 33
File Transfer Protocol (FTP), 114
firmware, 114
first job, viii
FORTRAN (FORmula TRANslator
    system), 21, 114
fourth-generation computers, 33
FTP (File Transfer Protocol), 114
function, 114
functional programming, 114

G
G2G3, 49
Getty Images, 52

Google, Inc., 45, 52
Google Apps, 37
graphical user interface, 114
graphics/multimedia, key
    positions in, 76–79
    animation/special effects
        programmer, 76–77
    computer game designer
        /programmer, 77
    computer graphic artist, 77
    electronic sound producer,
        77–78
    multimedia developer
        /producer, 78
    multimedia/game writer
        /editor, 78
    virtual reality designer
        /programmer, 78–79
"green" computing, 114–115
green IT, 37–38

H
hacking, 115
hardware, 115
hardware development, computer
    history and, 8–14
help desk, 128
history, computer, 1–25
    beginning of computing and,
        2–5
    chronology of landmark
        events in, 23–25
    hardware development, 8–14
    Internet development in,
        14–15, 17
    personal computers and, 9,
        10–13, 64
    term "computer" and, 1–2
    twentieth-century
        developments in, 5–8
    World Wide Web in, 17–23
hobbyists, computer history and, 9
honesty, accountability and,
    97–98, 108

Horn clause, 115
HTML (Hypertext Markup Language), 71, 115
HTTP (Hypertext Transfer Protocol), 115
hybrid languages, 20
HyperCard, 17
hypertext, 17, 115

I

IBM (International Business Machines), 45
IBM personal computer, 12
identifier, 115
If You *See* What I Mean (ISWIM), 21
Ifrah, Georges, 4, 14
imperative languages, 18–19
index (v), 115
industry analyst, 79–80
industry crossover, 102, 105
industry jargon, business language terms and, 109–124
Infante, Ramon (Ray), 46–47
Information Processing Language (IPL) (1956), 20
information systems operation/ management, key positions in, 61–66
    chief information officer, 61
    chief technology officer, 62
    computer security specialist, 62
    database administrator, 62–63
    information systems director, 63–64
    information systems manager, 64–65
    network/systems administrator, 65
    quality assurance specialist, 65–66
information technology (IT), 51
    green, 37–38

Information Technology Infrastructure Library (ITIL), 115
ink cartridges, 75
instance, 115
insurance carriers industry, 28, 30, 31
integrated circuits, 9, 15, 115–116
Intel Corporation, 10
interactive textiles, touch-sensitive, 15
International Business Machines (IBM), 11, 12
Internet, 37, 116, 129
    development, 14–15, 17
    languages, 20
    newspapers and, 69
    security, 3, 64, 70, 127
    standards, 104, 127
    Web 2.0 and, 39–50
    World Wide Web history and, 17–23
Internet advertising designer, 69–70
Internet applications programmer, 70–71
Internet service provider (ISP), 71
Internet store manager /entrepreneur, 71–72
Internet/Web site positions, 69–73
    Internet advertising designer, 69–70
    Internet service provider, 71
    Internet store manager /entrepreneur, 71–72
    Web site designer, 72–73
    Webmaster, 72
interviews
    Croly, Roberta, 100–101
    Infante, Ramon (Ray), 46–47
    Review Board certification, 102
    Short, Rob, 16
    Weiss, Bill 19
IP telephony, 116

IPL (Information Processing
    Language), 20
ISP. *See* Internet service provider
ISWIM (If You *See* What I
    Mean), 21 IT. *See* information
    technology
ITIL (Information Technology
    Infrastructure Library), 115

J
Jacquard, Joseph-Marie, 4–5
Java, 22
JavaScript, 22
job(s)
    changing, 83–84, 93–96
    defining ideal, 95
    interviews, 95–96
    losing, x
job descriptions. *See* key positions
job interviews, 95–96
    eye contact in, 100
    Microsoft CTO on, 100–101
Jobs, Steve, vii–viii
    firing of, x

K
Kenbak-1, 10–11
kernel, 116
key positions, 54–82
    computer-related office,
    80–82
    graphics/multimedia, 76–79
    information systems operation
        /management, 61–66
    Internet/web site, 69–73
    manufacturing, 73–76
    programming/software
        development, 54–61
    specialist positions as, 79–80
    training/support, 66–69
key skills, identifying, 93–94
    transferable, 94
keyboards, invention of, 14
kilobyte, 116

L
language, 116
languages, computer
    programming, 18–23. *See also*
    industry jargon, business
    language terms and
        certification in, 103
    computer programmers and,
        56–57
    generations of, 18, 33
    history of user-interface
        development, 9, 11
    Internet applications, 71
    natural, 118
    object-oriented, 19, 27–28, 85
    top, viii
laptop computers, 17, 40, 70, 116
lazy evaluation, 116
Licklider, J. C. R., 15
linear equation, 116
LinkedIn, 89
links, SLATES feature of Web 2.0,
    39
Linux, 41
LISt Processing, 21
log, 116
logarithm, 116
logic programming, 20, 116
LogLogic, 49
loom, mechanical, 4–5
loop, 116
Lovelace, Ada, 56

M
machine languages, 18
macro, 117
Macromedia. *See* Adobe Flash,
    certification by
magnetic core memory, 117
mainframe, 117
malware, 117
management of companies
    /enterprises sector
        computer programmers in, 28

network/systems
  administrators in, 32
software engineers in, 31
support specialists in, 35
systems analysts in, 30
manufacturing, key positions in,
  73–76
  computer hardware designer
    /engineer, 74
  computer hardware
    manufacturing technician,
    74
  computer systems designer,
    74–75
  computer-aided design
    technician/manager, 73
  computer-aided
    manufacturing technician,
    73–74
  embedded systems designer,
    75–76
  robotics engineer/technician,
    76
Margolis, Jane, 52
Mark I, first large-scale digital, 6–7
marketing specialist, 80
markup languages, 20
Master Series certification,
  Microsoft, 102
Mauchly, John, 7–8
McAfee, Andrew, 39
McCarthy, John, 36, 37
McCarthy, Joseph, 8
mechanical loom, 4–5
media resources, for training
  /certification, 136–139
memory, 10, 12, 97, 117
mentor, ix
method, 117
microcomputers, first, 9
microprocessors, 9, 10, 12, 14
Microsoft Corporation, 16
  Croly on style recognition in,
    100–101

statistics on, 46
Microsoft Corporation certification
  programs, 99–103
  database administrator, 87
  five levels available through,
    101
  Review Board interview in,
    102–103
  server engineer, 87
middleware, 117
Moore, Gordon, 10
Moore's law, 117
Mosaic, 17
Moss, Anne, 52
motherboard, 118
multimedia, 118
multiprocessing, 118
multitasking, 118
myths, PC, 64

N

National Bureau of Standards,
  U.S., 8
natural language, 118
netbook, 118
.NET Framework, 118
Netscape, 17
network, 118
network engineers, starting
  salaries for, 32
networking, viii, 89
network/systems administrators, 65
  employment/wage statistics
    on, 32
neural network, 118
newspapers, Internet and, 69
NextPlane, 49
node, 119
Noyce, Robert, 10
null pointer, 29

O

object-oriented programming, 19,
  27–28, 85, 119

office positions. *See* computer-
related office positions
Open Group, 129
open-source computer
programming, 119
open-source office suite, 42
operator, 119
overloading, 120
Oracle Corporation, 47–48, 103
SAP AG lawsuit and, 48
Osborne 1, first laptop computer,
17
outsourcing, 27, 29, 34, 52–53

P
packaged software, 57
packet, 120
packet switching, 14, 15, 120
Palo Alto Research Center (PARC),
11
Pascal, Blaise, 4, 14, 21, 25
Pascal, language, 21
passion, for technology, 43, 98,
106
passwords, 70
peripheral device, 120
Perl (Practical Extracting and
Report Language), 22
personal computers (PCs), 9,
10–13, 64
Personal Home Pages Hypertext
Processor, 22
personality traits, helpful
computer programmers, 85–86
computer support specialist, 93
database administrator, 89–90
software engineer, 88
systems analyst, 86–87
Web site designer, 92
phishing, 120
Pixar Animation Studios, x
podcast, 120
processor, 120
productivity, 42, 57

Professional Series certification,
Microsoft, 102
program, 120
programmers, 28, 56–57
animation/special effects,
76–77
applications, 28, 57
artificial intelligence, 55
computer, 26–28, 56–57,
84–86
engineering, 58–59
Internet applications, 70–71
systems, 57, 60–61
virtual reality designer and,
78–79
programming errors, Internet
security and, 3
programming/software
development, key positions in,
54–61
artificial intelligence
programmer, 55
bioinformatics specialist,
55–56
computer programmers, 56–57
data miner, 58
database analyst, 57–58
engineering programmer,
58–59
overview, 54–55
software engineer, 59
systems consultant, 60
systems programmer, 60–61
pseudo-viruses, 64
"pull" technology, 120
"push" technology, 120

Q
quantum mechanical computing,
38–39

R
random access memory (RAM),
10, 97

R&D. *See* research and
  development
read-only memory (ROM), 12, 97
recursivity, 120–121
register (n), 121
relational database, 121
relay (n), 121
reputation, professional, 96–98,
  107–108
research and development (R&D),
  43
resources, 136–139
  associations/organizations,
    125–130
  books/periodicals, 130–136
  computer industry web sites,
    140
  education, 138–139
résumé, 121
ROM. *See* read-only memory
routine, 121

S

SaaS (Software as a Service), 37,
  41, 121
sales representatives/managers, 80
SANS (SysAdmin, Audity,
  Network, Security) Institute, 3
SAP AG, Oracle lawsuit against, 48
Scala, 23
scripting languages, 20
Scriptwriter-Oriented Language, 23
search engine optimization (SEO),
  121
search, SLATES feature of Web
  2.0, 39
security, computer/Internet, 3, 64,
  70, 127
Selker, Ted, 42
Sendall, Mike, 17
SEO (search engine optimization),
  121
server engineers, certification for,
  87

Short, Rob, 16, 84, 97
signals, SLATES feature of Web
  2.0, 39
Silicon Valley, 121
skills/qualifications. *See also*
  education/skill requirements;
  key skills, identifying business
  communication techniques and,
  106–108
SLATES, Web 2.0 features, 39
SmallTalk, 21
SNOBOL (StroNg Oriented sym-
  BOlic Language), 21
Society of Women Engineers, 129
software, 121
  packaged, 57
Software & Information Industry
  Association, 130
Software as a Service (SaaS), 37,
  41, 121
software developers
  employment/wage statistics
    for, 28
  industry sectors employing,
    26–27
  starting salaries of, 28
software engineer, 59
  applications, 31
  career advancement, 87
  certification of, 87
  education/skill requirements
    for, 87
  employment/wage statistics
    on, 30–31
  personality traits helpful to,
    88
Software Engineering Institute,
  130
software publishers industry
  computer programmers in, 28
  software engineers in, 31
  support specialists in, 35
spam, e-mail, 94
specialist positions, 79–80

industry analyst, 79–80
marketing specialist, 80
sales representatives
/managers, 80
speed, computer, 13–14
spyware, 121
SQL (Standard Query Language),
22, 103
Standard Query Language (SQL),
22, 103
standards, Internet, 104, 127
state governments, network
/systems administrators working
for, 32
statistics, major companies and,
43–48
stereotypes, "geek," xv
StroNg Oriented symBOlic
Language (SNOBOL), 21
subroutine, 122
success, three requirements for,
106
Sun Microsystems, 13
Sureau, Denis L., 20
switch (n), 122
SysAdmin, Audity, Network,
Security (SANS) institute, 3
system, 122
systems analyst
certification of, 87
education/skill requirements
for, 86
employment/wage statistics,
28–30
industry sectors employing,
30
personality traits helpful to,
86–87

T
technical support positions, 66–67
technical writer/editor, 68–69
technology exposition, 50
passion for, 43

"pull"/"push," 120
Technology Series, Microsoft
certification, 102
technology trends/future trends,
42–43
telecommunications, 50, 122
TeleType machine, 122
Telnet, 122
textiles, touch-sensitive
interactive, 15
Theurk, Gary, 94
time management, 106–108
time sharing, 122
Torres y Quevedo, Leonardo, 5
Torvalds, Linus, 41
trade shows, 51
training
certification and, 102
media resources for, 136–139
training/support positions, 66–69
service technician, 67
software applications trainer,
67–68
technical editor, 68–69
technical support manager,
66–67
technical support specialist,
66–67
technical writer, 68
telecommunications
technician/engineer, 69
transferable skills, 94
transistors, 8, 9, 122
Transmission Control Protocol
/Internet Protocol (TCP/IP), 122
trends, computer industry
conferences and, 50–52
employment/wages, 26–35
future, 35–39
major companies and, 41–50
up/coming companies,
48–49
Web 2.0, 39–50
women in, 52–53

Trojan horse, 64, 123
Turing, Alan, 6, 25, 36
Turing Test, 36

U
UML (Unified Modeling
    Language), 22
UNIVAC (Universal Automatic
    Computer), 8, 33
UNIX, 123
*Unlocking the Clubhouse: Women in
    Computing* (Fisher/Margolis),
    52
user-interface
    browsing and, 17
    computer generations and, 33
    design, 61
    development, 9, 11
utility computing, 37

V
VA (Veterans' Administration)
    hospitals, 2
vacuum tubes, 8
Veterans' Administration (VA)
    hospitals, 2
videocast, 123
virtual communities, 17, 37
virus, 64, 123
    first computer "bug," 110
    worm v., 124
VoiceCon, annual conference, 51
von Leibniz, Gottfried Wilhelm,
    4
von Neumann, John, 6

W
WAN (wide area network), 123
WC3 (World Wide Web
    Consortium), 104, 124
Web 2.0, 39–50
    SLATES features of, 39
Web browser, 17–18, 123

Webinar, 123
Webmaster, 72
Web site designers, 72–73
    certification of, 103–105
    education/skill requirements
        for, 90–92
    employment/wage statistics
        on, 33–34
    personality traits helpful to,
        92
Web sites, industry resources,
    140
WebYoda's Online Webmaster
    (WOW), 103
Weiss, Bill, 19, 98
WHO (World Health
    Organization), 56
Wicker, Scott, 75
wide area network (WAN), 123
Wi-Fi, 123
Windows Core Technology,
    Microsoft, 84
Winsome Trading, 48
wired telecommunications
    carriers industry, network
    /systems administrators in,
    32
WITSA (World Information
    Technology and Services
    Alliance), 40
women, in computer industry,
    52–53, 56, 125, 126, 129
Woodard, Darcey, 48, 53
workaholic, 98
World Health Organization
    (WHO), 56
World Information Technology
    and Services Alliance (WITSA),
    40
world market, computer industry
    and, 40–41
World Wide Web
    history of, 17–23

precursor of, 17
World Wide Web Consortium
   (WC3), 104, 124, 130
worm, 124, 137
WOW (WebYoda's Online
   Webmaster), areas of, 103–104

X
Xavier-Thomas, Charles, 14

Z
Zink imaging, 75
zombies, 3